John S Webber

In and Around Cape Ann

A Hand-book of Gloucester, Mass. and its immediate vicinity - For the wheelman tourist and the summer visitor

John S Webber

In and Around Cape Ann
A Hand-book of Gloucester, Mass. and its immediate vicinity - For the wheelman tourist and the summer visitor

ISBN/EAN: 9783337192945

Printed in Europe, USA, Canada, Australia, Japan

Cover: Foto ©Andreas Hilbeck / pixelio.de

More available books at **www.hansebooks.com**

A HAND-BOOK OF

Gloucester, Mass., and Its Immediate Vicinity.

FOR THE

Wheelman Tourist and the Summer Visitor,

BY

JOHN S. WEBBER, JR.,

B. BI. C., CONSUL C. T. C.

———

WITH ELEVEN ILLUSTRATIONS.

"I have always counted a run to Gloucester as one of the finest in New England, and never omit it when in the vicinity of Salem, if my time will allow."—C. A. HAZLETT

———

GLOUCESTER, MASS.:
PRINTED AT THE CAPE ANN ADVERTISER OFFICE,
1885.

TO

H. W. GRIMES, ESQ.,

CONSUL C. T. C.,

GLOUCESTER, GLOUCESTER COUNTY, ENGLAND,

THIS LITTLE VOLUME IS MOST RESPECTFULLY DEDICATED

BY

JOHN S. WEBBER, JR.,

CONSUL C. T. C.,

GLOUCESTER, MASSACHUSETTS, U. S. A.

A Word at the Start.

After months of labor—hard labor, too, for one unaccustomed to the work—I am permitted to send forth the present little manual on Gloucester, and its immediate vicinity. The material here given is designed for the especial use of the touring wheelman and the summer visitor, and I have endeavored to describe—in a way perhaps peculiar—all the most important sights and places of interest to be found upon this rock-bound territory of Cape Ann.

Much of the historical matter in Part I has been written up from suggestions found in various publications, to wit: History of Gloucester, History of Essex County, Fisherman's Memorial and Record Book, etc., to the authors of which I desire to tender my grateful acknowledgments; the files of the Cape Ann *Advertiser* and Cape Ann *Bulletin* have also been occasionally referred to for dates and other valuable items.

I am not unmindful of the many kind favors extended by various friends, and would therefore thank especially Mr. J. J. Gilligan of Boston, C. A. Hazlett, Esq., of Portsmouth, N. H., Mr. H. Frank Sanford of Gloucester, Mr. George Holliday of the Masconomo Hotel, Mrs. E. S. Robinson of the Pigeon Cove House, Mr. George L. Smith of the Gloucester Hotel, Mr. William P. Davis of the Pavilion Hotel, and all others who have in any way aided me in the preparation of the present volume.

The beautiful pictures that adorn the following pages (with the exception of the four hotel cuts) were made expressly for the work from photographs, by the Photo. Electro. Eng. Co., 20 Cliff street, New York, and those of our friends who are familiar with the locations will readily recognize the correctness of the views.

J. S. W., Jr.

GLOUCESTER, MASS., July, 1885.

CONTENTS.

	Page.
A Word at the Start,	3

PART I.

Concerning Gloucester,	5

PART II.

I.	Bicycle Rambles on Eastern Point,	26
II.	Saunterings at Magnolia,	32
III.	By Wheel to Chebacco Pond,	41
IV.	A Wheel Around Cape Ann,	50
V.	Coffin's Beach,	66
VI.	Manchester-by-the Sea,	71

PART III.

I.	Miscellaneous,	78
II.	A Wheel Run in '78,	83
III.	Wheelmen Visitors in Past Years,	88

LIST OF ILLUSTRATIONS.

I.	GLOUCESTER HOTEL,	Frontispiece.
II.	PAVILION BEACH,	Opposite page 20
III.	VIEW FROM BELLEVUE,	" " 24
IV.	BASS ROCK HOUSE,	" " 29
V.	VIEW ON 'SQUAM RIVER,	" " 45
VI.	PIGEON COVE HOUSE,	" " 53
VII.	FOLLY COVE,	" " 58
VIII.	DAVIS' NECK, FROM GEN. BUTLER'S,	" " 60
IX.	WILLOW ROAD, RIVERDALE,	" " 64
X.	COFFIN'S BEACH,	" " 68
XI.	PAVILION HOTEL,	" " 78

PART I.

CONCERNING GLOUCESTER.

Any map of Massachusetts will show plainly where Cape Ann is. Away up in the most northeast corner you will easily find this prominent headland jutting out into the sea, the waters of Massachusetts Bay washing its southern shore, those of Ipswich Bay its northern, and the waves of the broad Atlantic its eastern, while the towns of Essex and Manchester form its western boundary.

The town of Gloucester comprised originally the entire peninsula of Cape Ann, but in 1840 the section on its eastern extremity known as "Sandy Bay," with a population of nearly twenty-seven hundred souls, was set off by an act of the Legislature under the name of Rockport, and became a separate town.

Cape Ann extends in an easterly direction from the main land about nine miles, and in width varies from three and one-half miles to nearly six. An arm of the sea, known as Annisquam River (or, as more frequently spoken, 'Squam River), extending from Ipswich Bay on the north to the harbor of Gloucester on the south, completely cuts the section into two nearly equal parts, with the business portion of the city on the eastern side.

Gloucester harbor, formed by the projection of a narrow strip of land in a southwesterly direction, is well known as one of the finest, and in many respects most convenient, on the northeast coast, affording, as it does, within its friendly embrace, safe anchorage and shelter for a large fleet. In the months of September and October, on a dusky night, the spectacle is most magnificent, when perhaps half a thousand sail of vessels are riding calmly at anchor with lights sparkling brightly from their positions on board.

Annisquam harbor, on the north, is very conveniently situated, but a bar across its entrance makes it difficult of access for other than the small fishing and pleasure craft belonging in the immediate vicinity.

About the year 1626 the first settlement was made at Gloucester, which in 1639 was incorporated as a "fishing plantation," and three years after became a town. In the year 1873 the town, with about sixteen thousand inhabitants, was granted its city charter. The name "Gloucester" was probably taken from the English town of that name, from which many of our earlier settlers came.

As a matter of record (for I am confident the article has never before appeared in type) I append a complete copy of the original document the town government received from the Indian, Samuel English, in the year 1700, whereby that personage relinquished to the inhabitants all right or title he then had in the territory now occupied by the city of Gloucester and the town of Rockport:

To ALL PEOPLE TO WHOM THESE PRESENTS SHALL COME Samuel English an Indian, the Grandson and Rightfull heir of Masshanomett the Sacamore of Agawam, Sendeth Greeting. Know yee that I the said Samuel English Sufficient reasons moving me thereunto but especially for ye full and just summe of seven pounds of Current money of New England truly paid unto me by Lieut. William Stevens and Ensign Joseph Allen a Committee or agents for ye towne of Glosster in the County of Essex in New England, wherewith I ye said Samuel English doo hereby acknowledge myself fully satisfied paid and content forever and thereof, and of every part thereof, doo hereby for me, my heirs executors and administrators forever acquit release and discharge them the said Committee their heirs executors & administrators forever. Have given granted bargained sold and confined and doo by these presents for myself heirs executors & administrators for ever grant Bargain Sell and Confine forever unto them the said William Stevens & Joseph Allen in their behalfe & for use and property of said Towne of Glosster them their heirs executors administrators and assigns forever a Certaine Tract of land knowne by ye name of ye Township of Glosster in the County aforesaid in New England Containing by estimation Ten thousand acres, be the Contents thereof more or less as it is abutted and bounded north northwest by Ipswich and West southwest by ye Towne of Manchester according as ye Lines hath been already settled & by ye salt sea on all other parts with all ye Islands thereto belonging according to ye grant of ye General Court to said Towne. Together with all ye Lands, Soyles, waters, rivers, streams havens, ports Fishing huntings Wood Timber Stones grass feed and all ye rights profits priviledges and appurtenances belonging to ye same or any part thereof. To Have and To Hold to them ye said William Stevens & Joseph Allen and ye said Towne of Glosster them their heirs executors administrators and assigns in quiet & peaceabe possession for ever without the Least lett, hindrance or molestation whatsoever & further I the said Samuel English doo hereby promise covenant and grant to & with ye abovesaid William Stevens and Joseph Allen that at & untill the ensealing and delivery of these presents I had good rightfull power and Lawfull authority to give grant convey and confirm the said premises and every part thereof with all the appurtenances as abovesaid, it Naturally decending to me from my predecessor as above said and doo hereby bind myselfs heirs, executors administrators and assigns Forever to defend ye said William Stevens and Joseph Allen and the said Towne of Glosster, Them Their heirs executors administrators and assigns for ever from all Indian right and Title & from The lawfull claims of all persons whatsoever to ye abovesaid premises. In witness whereof I ye abovesaid Samuel English doo hereunto set my hand & seal this fourteenth day of January seventeen hundred & in ye 12 yeare of his Magistys reighn.

SAMUEL $\overset{his}{\underset{marke}{\times}}$ ENGLISH [Seal.]

Signed Sealed & Delivered in presence of us

ABRAHAM PERKINS }
JOSEPH FFOSTER }
JONA FAIRBANKS }

The within mentioned Samuel English personally appearing before me the subscriber one of ye Members of his Mag'y counsell for the Province of ye Mass. Bay & Justice of peace in the same, acknowledged thee within written Instrument to be his free act and deed.

JOHN APPLETON.

EARLY SCHOOLS.

Gloucester began the erection of suitable buildings for educational purposes in the year 1708, when the first school house in town of which there is any record was built on the easterly side of "Meeting House Green," so called, in the Town Parish. The dimensions were—24 feet in length, 16 feet in width and 6 feet in stud. The cost was 24£ 15s. A grant of 300£ was made in the year 1793 for the building of a grammar school house, at the suggestion of Rev. Eli Forbes. This building stood on what is now Granite street, and was a square two-story edifice with belfry and bell. For sixty years the building remained in this locality, and was then removed to Beacon street, and is now used as a primary school. Nearly one-fifth of the entire population of Gloucester are school children: The High school enrolls over 159 names, the Grammar 2200, and the Mixed and Primary about 1800, and her schools for the last ten years have cost the city nearly $550,000.

The banking business of Gloucester is well represented in the four National and one Savings institutions, and commenced as long ago as the year 1795, when the first meeting called for the purpose of establishing some sort of banking institution in town was held at the insurance office of Fitz & Ignatius Sargent—a small building standing on the corner of what are now Duncan and Main streets. At this meeting a committee consisting of Daniel Rogers, David Plumer, John Somes, William Pearson and Col. William Pearce, was appointed to consider the expediency of such an institution and to make report. The report was rendered at a meeting held the first day of January in 1796, and was in favor of the establishing of a bank of $40,000 capital, with no stockholder less than $100 or more than $4,000. This was the first banking institution in town, and was called the "Gloucester Bank," and John Somes was its first president. The committee appointed January 12, 1796, "to look for a suitable place to keep a bank," spent a long time in seeking a convenient building, without success, and then decided to purchase the vacant lot in front of Capt. Babson's dwelling house and build their own edifice. The building erected was a one-story wooden affair, with an entrance on the westerly side through a small yard leading from the street. The bank occupied the room nearest the street, and the board of directors the one in the rear. The vault of the new institution was of stone and situated under the banking room in a place excavated for the purpose, and was reached by a stairway, to which access was had through a heavy trap-door, which was raised by a tackle attached to the ceiling. In these new quarters the bank did business for nearly thirty-five years and then removed to their new stone building opposite the foot of Short street, on what is now Main street, and in this edifice continued business for forty years. The business center of the town then changing to the vicinity of the Custom House caused the bank in the year 1871 to erect the brick structure now occupied by it on the corner of Main and Duncan streets.

THE FIRST SCHOONER.

It was at Gloucester that the name "schooner," which we now hear so frequently spoken, had its origin, as appears by current traditions of the town. Certain it is that the word was unknown previous to the year 1713—in fact, little or nothing is known about the vessels used on the New England coast previous to that time. For the benefit of those to whom the story has not been told I will append it here, according to Mr. Babson, the historian of the town: "It seems that Capt. Andrew Robinson, a citizen of the town, and famous for his ingenuity, built a vessel in the year 1713 and masted and rigged it in a peculiar manner. When the vessel was launched, and as she was sliding off the stocks, a bystander cried out, 'How she scoons!' and Capt. Robinson instantly remarked, 'A schooner let her be.' Thus was the new name created in our marine vocabulary. The craft was rigged nearly the same as are our vessels of to-day, and the name of 'schooner' has always clung to them from the date mentioned."

The chief business of Gloucester is, and always was, as any one must by this time be well aware, that of fishing. This business, now so important as to place the city first in rank in the world, employs over six hundred vessels, and is actively pursued at all seasons of the year. The total product in value of the fisheries for the year 1828 was $250,000; for 1847 about $600,000; and for 1883 about $4,500,000. These figures are based on careful estimates founded mostly on exact returns. Nearly all our fishermen who bring this large amount of wealth into port are of foreign birth, and a large majority of them have only a temporary home in our city, and considering the temptations to which, more than men of other employments, they are exposed, it may be truly said that in manners and morals they will well stand a comparison with any other class of society. For one great quality they are pre-eminently conspicuous—for what but the stoutest heart could brave the dangers and hardships of an employment, in which during the last twenty-five years *over seventeen hundred* men have passed through appalling scenes of storm and sea and shipwreck to a watery grave!

Let me append the record of the last ten years of the disasters in the Gloucester fisheries, as gleaned from the columns of the *Cape Ann Advertiser*, the best authority on matters appertaining to this industry of fishing:

YEAR.	VESSELS.	TONNAGE.	VALUE.	INSURANCE.	LIVES.
1875	16	1,050.91	$96,000	$81,326	123
1876	27	1,075.46	150,000	116,222	212
1877	8	722.33	45,000	22,000	39
1878	13	907.57	64,794	49,067	56
1879	29	1,893.36	111,056	90,582	249
1880	7	360.44	21,000	15,972	52
1881	8	511.51	31,000	20,493	56
1882	12	976.74	79,700	54,460	115
1883	17	1,119.27	94,400	76,972	209
1884	16	1,104.46	87,100	63,100	131
Total.	153	9,722.05	$780,050	$590,194	1242
Average,	15	972.20	$78,005	$59,019	124

For more particular information concerning the fisheries and the terrible dangers attending them, the reader is referred to the valuable works of George H. Procter, Esq., entitled, "The Fishermen's Memorial and Record Book," and "The Fishermen's Own Book," both published by Procter Brothers, of this city.

THE SOUTHERN MACKEREL SEINERS.

I would like to say a few words concerning the business of the Southern mackerel seiners—a business that has especially grown to considerable extent during the last few years.

Every Spring witnesses the fitting out and sailing of a large fleet of Gloucester vessels for the southern waters, sometimes the trip extending as far south as the Carolina capes. These vessels market their trips, first at the Philadelphia and New York markets, and late in the season at Boston and this city. Considerable rivalry on the part of half a dozen of our "crack" skippers, as to which would land the first trip, has made the business of an early departure and quick return a prominent feature of the season's work.

The business of seining fish around a vessel is one so little understood by the uninitiated, that perhaps it may be of interest to quote a writer in the *Cape Ann Bulletin* of a recent date:

"It is a well known fact that, at times, for days, and sometimes weeks, no mackerel are to be seen 'schooling' at the surface of the water, although that they are present on the fishing ground can be easily proven by heaving a vessel to and 'throwing bait' for a short time, when the fish will rise from the depths and remain alongside of the vessel as long as the operation of feeding is continued. Again, when making their passage, in coming north or in returning to their winter haunts, the fish are sometimes very difficult to catch, even though swimming near the surface of the sea, for the reason that they generally travel at a rapid rate ; and by scattering bait across their line of travel and heaving the vessel to, they can be stopped, though sometimes but for a few moments. At such times seiners take care to keep the seine boat in readiness on the port side of the vessel (the leeward side when hove to), hauled up snug to the vessel, that no delay may be had if mackerel rise in sufficient quantities to warrant the setting of the seine. It requires but a word from the master, if they do rise, when away go the men into the boat, followed by the skipper, a spare hand or the cook taking the place at the bait box and continuing to throw the 'food for the fishes.' The boat is in the meanwhile dropped around on the starboard quarter, and when about twenty fathoms off, overboard goes the end of the seine with buoy attached, which is picked up and held by two men in the seine dory, and the boat is pulled to leeward at right angles with the vessel, as fast as the seine can be got out, as much depends on getting to leeward as far as possible, as the vessel is constantly changing her position, driven by wind and wave. When the middle of the seine is reached (usually marked by a double canvas-covered cork) the boat is turned short around and all possible speed made up to and across the vessel's bow, and, with another sharp turn, straight to the dory. As soon as the operation of 'pursing,' or drawing the bottom of the seine together, is commenced, the man in charge of the vessel quickly scatters several buckets of bait into the water, in order to keep the unsuspecting victims of man's wants busy, then springs to the fore-sheet and hauls it in ; up goes the jib ; the wheel, which has been hard down, is righted, the vessel pays off, and gathering headway, is soon speeding over the cork-ropes out of the centre of the seine, the ropes and seine sinking and going beneath the vessel at right angles to the keel, leaving the mackerel behind. If the operation of getting headway on the vessel is not skilfully done and she be allowed to drift broadside to the ropes, there is danger of catching the seine, and then good-bye to the fish, for that time at least, with a prospect of mending to be done to repair damages. When once outside of the seine the man in charge of the vessel has only to keep clear of the boat and sail at his own sweet will and pleasure until the fish are 'dried up' (all the slack twine being in the boat and the fish in close quarters in the bunt), which fact is learned by observing an oar upheld by some one on board the boat. Perhaps at the last moment, before the closing of the seine, the fish have escaped, when, with sore hands and tired body, we, remembering the old adage, prepare to 'try, try, try again,' or mayhaps, as I have seen the case, from one barrel to over two hundred of the shining beauties are secured and are soon tumbling over the rail from the big dip net, and the hearts of the fisher lads are made glad, even though the prospect of an all night and day job at dressing and salting be in prospect."

In the early days the boats engaged in the shore fishery occasionally marketed a few barrels of fresh mackerel at Boston, but no particular notice was taken at that time as to the possible prospective value of this fishery until a few years later, in 1821, when the adjacent bay became the schooling ground for large numbers of them. The fishermen then built especial vessels, and devoted considerable time to the taking of this particular fish. Every Summer was the business pursued, and the success was far beyond their expectations; in a couple of years the vessels of the Gloucester fleet marketed over 120,000 barrels. The boats were known by the name of "jiggers," and carried from six to eight men. In 1825 one of these jiggers took over 1300 barrels.

The growth of Cape Ann may be attributed to a considerable extent to the influence of her newspapers, the earliest of which, the *Gloucester Telegraph*, appeared in January, 1827, with W. E. P. Rogers as its publisher, and was a sheet 28x20 inches, with twenty columns of reading matter. In 1842 Mr. John S. E. Rogers began the publication of the *Cape Ann Light*, and also assumed control of the *Telegraph*, the former appearing once and the latter twice a week. In 1848 Mr. John J. Piper began the issuing of the *Gloucester News*, which Mr. Rogers afterwards purchased and merged into the *Telegraph*. In 1874 the *Telegraph* came into the hands of Mr. M. V. B. Perley, and was conducted by him until 1876, when the publication ceased. In 1877 its successor was established by Messrs. Woodbury, Low & Co., under the title, *Cape Ann Bulletin*, which paper, now in the hands of Messrs. Haskell & Tresilian, is still alive and wide-awake.

In the month of August, 1884, the publication of the *Cape Ann Evening Breeze* was begun at the *Bulletin* office, which has since enjoyed a prosperous career, as has also the *Gloucester Daily News*, a publication introduced about a couple of months previous to the appearance of the *Breeze*, by Messrs. F. A. Wiggin & Co.

In July, 1853, Messrs. Francis & George H. Procter started a gratuitous monthly, 28x22 inches, headed, *The Able Sheet;* in January, 1854, its size was enlarged to 22x34 inches, and until the year 1855 was printed at the *Telegraph* office. In January, 1855, the proprietors changed the name to the *Gloucester Advertiser*, and issued the paper from their own establishment. In July, 1857, its publication twice a month began, and its subscription price was 75 cents per year. In December of the same year the name was changed to the *Cape Ann Advertiser*, and it made its appearance fortnightly. In 1858 it was made a weekly, and their firm name changed to Procter Brothers. The paper was enlarged in 1865 to 27x42 inches, and in 1882 assumed its present size, 29x42 inches. Characterized by liveliness, energy and determination to excel, the sheet is justly entitled to the liberal patronage bestowed upon it by its five thousand subscribers.

MANUFACTURES.

The manufactures of Gloucester cannot be said to be especially prominent, and such as the city does enjoy are naturally closely allied to her main business. The recently organized Net and Twine Company, at its place of business near the railroad station, employs a large force of workmen, and makes the manufacture of seines, twines, &c., a specialty.

The Cape Ann Anchor Works is another large concern, situated near the railroad bridge on 'Squam river, employing night and day gangs of men the year round, the particular work of this company being the manufacture of anchors, car axles and other heavy iron work.

The large building on the opposite side of the railroad and also upon the river bank, is the headquarters of the Gloucester Fish Drying Company, organized in 1884.

The Russia Cement Company, on Essex avenue, and the Gloucester Isinglass and Glue Company, on Eastern avenue, enjoy a good business in their line of fish glues and cements.

Other prominent business establishments are those of Lewis H. Merchant, near the Net and Twine Company's building, in the manufacture of fish boxes, &c.; Higgins & Gifford, boat builders, at the "head of the harbor"; A. W. Dodd & Co.. cod liver, oil, &c.; and the machine shop of Nathan Richardson on

Washington street, where the bicyclist will find competent workmen to repair any slight damage to his wheel.

The wharves of the fishing firms will doubtless claim the first attention of the stranger guest, and a visit to the scene of the landing of a trip of fish is often of much interest to the beholder for the first time. The Atlantic Halibut Co.'s buildings on the way leading from Duncan street, and those of the New England Fish Co., on Dodd's wharf, and also the firm of Stockbridge & Co., on Parmenter, Rice & Co.'s wharf, are especial points of interest worthy a visit, the discharging of a trip of fresh halibut at either of these places is a sight of much enjoyment to the visitor, and should not be missed.

The wharves of Messrs. Cunningham & Thompson, John Pew & Son, Parmenter, Rice & Co., and Stanwood & Co., are among the most important in the business of boxing and putting up "boneless codfish" for table use. These firms employ a large force of male help and ship immense quantities of this particular fish in this form, and the operation of skinning and cutting is one of keen interest to the sightseer. This industry, which was started but a few years ago, has grown to such proportions that at the present time nine-tenths of all the dry fish shipped from this city is prepared in this way, and it is estimated that 25,000,000 pounds of boneless fish are sold each year, giving employment to three hundred laborers all the year 'round, with a payroll amounting to something like an hundred thousand dollars per annum. In the production of this vast amount of marketable goods some 5000 tons of waste material remain to be disposed of in some way. Formerly this refuse was given to any one who would cart it away, and much of it was spread upon the land to be ploughed under in the spring and to pollute the air of summer with its odor of decay; but gradually the demand for it increased, as it was found to be an excellent ingredient in the manufacture of guano, and to-day there is a ready market for every bit of this material.*

In the "Fishermen's Own Book" the Messrs. Procter give a particularly interesting sketch on page 133 relating to the chief industry of this city, which, with their kind permission, appears below :

"It is a lively scene, down at some of our wharves in the breezy days of midwinter, to witness one or more of the Bankers or Georgesmen round the Point and come gayly up the harbor. Sometimes they are minus a spar or sail and are all battered or iced up, the crew having had a hard time freeing the bows and rigging from the frozen spray, which in a bitter cold day hardens as soon as it strikes, and piles itself up on the overburdened craft with amazing quickness. Then the safety of the vessel and her management through the cold, seething waters, render it an imperative necessity that the ice be dislodged, and a cold, cheerless task it is which the fisherman has forced upon him. Short spells of this ice pounding, with the thermometer below zero, is all that men can endure, and they are frequently relieved, all hands taking their turn and making the best of an unwelcome duty. But snug in the harbor, anchor down, sails furled, pipes lighted, with the catch sold, the crew have a little resting spell. Then the vessel is hauled alongside the wharf of some of the fresh fish buyers, the hatches opened, and out from the depths below are hoisted the mammoth halibut, direct from the ice house, where they are kept as sweet and fresh as when first caught. Up they come in pairs, and sometimes in triplets, according to their size, and oftentimes a monster weighing two

---

* *Cape Ann Bulletin*, somewhat changed.

hundred pounds and upwards will show his nose above deck and be slowly landed on the wharf. Visions of nice fried or baked halibut tickle the palate, as the fish are thus landed. After their heads are taken off and the fish thoroughly cleansed and packed in boxes, the last thing done, ere they are nailed up, is to fill their napes with crushed ice, which insures their preservation, and off they are shipped by rail or steamer to Boston, New York, Philadelphia, Lowell and other large cities, where they find ready sales. The codfish are discharged mostly at the wharves of the vessel owners, where they are decapitated and then salted in butts, and when sufficiently salt are transferred to the flakes for a given time and dried. Then they find their way, the most of them, in these days, to the skinning lofts, where nimble fingers divest them of skin and bones, and the solid pieces of fish, handsome as can be, are packed in boxes from ten to two hundred pounds each, which find their way from the warehouses of our enterprising fish producers to all sections of this country. The trade is simply immense, and constantly on the increase, for the praise of the Gloucester boneless cod is abroad in the land, and dealers and consumers demand it from headquarters, direct from first hands.

Who would have thought, from the small beginning in the putting up of boneless codfish, of only a few years since, that such large results would follow? And now that fish is packed in such clean, attractive packages, the attention of consumers is drawn toward it. The old objection to stripping and cleaning, and purchasing so much waste, is heard no more. The clean fish, ready for a salt fish dinner or fish balls, is now for sale by all first-class grocers in the country, and the Gloucester brands, of which there are several hundred, each large purchaser having his private brands, are printed indelibly on the boxes. Some of these brands are very handsome and add much to the attractiveness of the packages.

The first man, Mr. George H. Smith, we think it was, who put up fish in this way, never dreamed that this act of his would revolutionize the entire fish trade, but so it has proved ! The old fish dealers, conservative, as they had a right to be, saw not the cloud which was rising, but kept in the old channels of shipping whole fish, until their customers demanded of them the boneless fish in boxes. And then they gave way to the inevitable. There was no help for it. Either adopt the new mode or lose the business altogether. And they entered into the business with the same energy which characterized their other transactions, and we have to-day, here in old Gloucester, a business which is now only in its infancy, a business which will keep the fleet busy, which will take all the fish they can catch, at remunerative prices, a business which will keep Gloucester in the front as a fishing port and furnish occupation for her people.

It's lively all through, from the time the vessel leaves the harbor until she arrives on the ground, and from the catching of the fish to the dressing, then the salting and drying, boning and skinning, shipping, and finally the serving up of the toothsome dish on the table with drawn butter and egg sauce, or the good old fashioned pork scraps, with beets and potatoes."

The sights around Gloucester, with the exception of those in the immediate vicinity of the wharves, as spoken of in the foregoing, are not particularly attractive, though our visiting bicycling friends may enjoy some of the more prominent of them, such as our public buildings, beaches, pleasant walks and drives, views of ocean scenery from the several high hill-tops, and a glance at the many natural curiosities to be found upon our Cape.

Pavilion Beach.

IN AND AROUND CAPE ANN.

On Dale avenue stands the beautiful City Hall, built in 1869 on the site of a former one burned the year previous. Bicyclists and other visitors to our city will find much of interest within this public building. Mr. Arthur C. Millett, the ever courteous "gentleman in charge," will cheerfully show you over the house, including the grand picture from the tower windows—a picture well looked upon from this standpoint being unsurpassed by any other within the city's limits, including as it does the entire settlement and adjacent country, with a most magnificent stretch of ocean scenery and the twin lighthouses on Thacher's Island, seemingly so near at hand. City Clerk Somes, at his office in this building, will be happy to give wheelmen any information sought by them in his department.

SAWYER FREE LIBRARY.

At the corner of Dale avenue and Middle street, a few yards from the City Hall, is the spacious and beautiful "Sawyer Free Library" building. These attractive grounds were purchased by Samuel E. Sawyer, Esq., for the purpose of establishing a permanent home for the library, in February of last year, of Mr. William A. Pew, for the sum of $20,000. The grounds of this noble mansion are extensive and well laid out, and Mr. Sawyer has spent large sums of money in fitting up the place for the purposes for which it is now used. The large rooms and stately halls are carpeted and elegantly furnished. The walls are adorned with over one hundred and fifty rare and valuable paintings and pictures, collected during Mr. Sawyer's visits to foreign cities and in this country. The generous donor has done everything that could be done to make the home of the library that bears his name convenient and beautiful. When the library was dedicated in July, 1884, a large assembly of our best citizens were present, together with several persons from abroad. Mr. Sawyer then presented to the trustees the deed of the entire property, comprising nearly 30,000 square feet of land, and thereby made it a perpetual gift to the citizens of Gloucester. The building was erected in 1764, and is consequently over 120 years old, though during that time it has been somewhat altered and improved by its several owners. Mr. Pew built the fine tower upon it and the verandas around the first story, and also the "porte cochere." He laid out the grounds with considerable taste, and protected them with the fine walls of dressed granite and iron gateways. Mr. Sawyer's improvements have embellished this valuable estate in many respects, and to-day it is one of the finest sites within our city. The rooms are open daily, afternoon and evening (except Tuesdays), from 2 to 5 and 7 to 9—Thursdays, in evening only. The library owns about 6500 volumes.

St. Ann's church (Roman Catholic), of which the Rev. J. J. Healy is pastor, is a handsome and substantial structure, at the corner of Smith and Park streets. The edifice is of stone, from the Rockport Granite Co., is Gothic in architecture, and measures one hundred and forty-two feet in length by eighty-three feet in width, with a spire one hundred and eighty-five feet in height. Within the church the beautifully frescoed walls and ceilings and the windows of stained glass present a very handsome effect. The altar is Gothic, and composed of the richly looking marble of the far away East. The two beautiful paintings here—one on the left of the main altar, and the other on the wall opposite—were executed under the direction of Father Healy at the Pitti Palace in Florence, Italy, and are both among the finest works of art in this country.

The rooms of the Cape Ann Scientific and Literary Association, in the City National Bank building, on Main street, are well worthy a visit. The Society has a fine collection of rare specimens, most of which were brought in by our vessels from deep-sea fishing trips.

The Young Men's Christian Association, in their new quarters on Main street (over Calef's dry goods store), have neatly fitted rooms, open at all times to the caller, and well supplied with reading matter for his entertainment.

A walk along Main street, the principal thoroughfare of the city, will give the visitor an idea of the business section of the place. On this street are the banks, custom house and post office, and nearly all the first-class retail stores.

The First Parish Church in Gloucester was built in 1738 on the same spot where the present Unitarian church now stands, on Middle street—adjacent to the Public Library grounds—and served the uses of the parish until 1828, when the present building was erected. It was this church that caused so much trouble to the sloop-of-war " Falcon," in 1775, by the constant ringing of its bell, warning the inhabitants of the approach of this pirate Lindsay and his crew. It seems Lindsay came into our harbor in pursuit of a vessel laden with West India products, and the town refused to aid him in the capture of the craft, but kept the bell in the church belfry clanging constantly as if in defiance of the " Falcon's " demands, which so enraged the pirate captain that he ordered his gunner to fire on "that d—n Presbyterian church," into the wall of which penetrated the ball now suspended in the vestibule of the present building, and which will always be preserved as an interesting relic of the exciting scene enacted so many long years ago.

A very pleasant locality for the stranger to visit is' Pavilion Beach, just off from Western avenue. Here one enjoys the ever welcome cooling sea breeze, and delights to sit and watch the motley gathering. The bathing facilities are excellent, and boats for a pleasant row around the harbor are also within easy reach.

"Stage Fort," just beyond the beach, on the Hough Farm property, is a grand place for pole-fishing and also a favorite spot for the rambling tourist. The old fortifications at this point were first built in 1812, and afterward reconstructed and occupied during the late rebellion.

The surface of the Cape is very uneven, and one almost wonders at the many huge, bold and precipitous ledges and rocky hills that confront him in every direction. Countless numbers of loose, shaggy masses of granite appear on either hand and are scattered thickly all over the entire territory. The highest elevation is in the West Parish, and is called Thompson's Mountain, being about two hundred and fifty feet above the sea level. From the top of this eminence the view on a clear day is superb. Bunker Hill Monument, Wachusett Mountain, and Monadnock can plainly be noticed, and with a glass you can catch a glimpse of old Agamenticus in the State of Maine.

Beacon Pole Hill, a prominent high elevation of land in the centre of the city, affords a fine view of the ocean and Annisquam river, and by glass of Ipswich bay, Newburyport and Portsmouth; in fact, a panoramic picture of unsurpassed beauty. This hill derives its name from the placing of a beacon, by the General Court, on its summit in the year 1776.

The streets about town are generally in condition for bicycle riding, though the surface of most of them is either cut up by thick patches of the coarsest gravel or a layer of loosely lying stones; the rider, however, can pick his way along without any very serious trouble. Main street is paved with square blocks

View from Bellevue, Showing City Farm and River.

of granite from Porter street to Hancock street, and from Chestnut street to Union Hill. Western avenue, or more frequently spoken of as the "Cut," is a favorite street for bicycle riding; beyond the bridge take the deserted sidewalk on the left, and enjoy a very pleasant spin upon its easy running surface.

Gloucester is divided into eight wards, and also contains several distinct villages, viz.: East Gloucester, in ward one, being the whole of the section known as Eastern Point; Magnolia, in ward eight, a tract of seashore property in the southwestern corner of the city; Lanesville and Bay View, in ward seven, on the northeast coast; Annisquam and Riverdale, in ward six, also in the northern section; West Gloucester, in ward eight; and the city proper, in wards two, three, four and five; each of which we shall have occasion to speak of hereafter.

PART II.

I—BICYCLE RAMBLES ON EASTERN POINT.

And now let's take our wheel for a short run along our harbor road to East Gloucester, and note the many points of interest on the way. The start is made at the Gloucester Hotel—the headquarters of all visiting wheelmen in this city—at the corner of Main and Washington streets; from thence the journey takes us over the rather uneven surface of Main street, going directly toward the east. In a few minutes we pass the Post Office on the left, and soon leave the noisy business portion of the street behind us, then, ere we are aware of it, we reach and quickly climb the slight eminence known as Union Hill. Once over the hill the road has a downward grade, with generally a very muddy surface, but on through this we propel our machine to the curve in the road at its junction with Eastern avenue. To the right we follow the now well trodden thoroughfare and again pedal quickly up the steep incline before us. Now the machine is well taken in hand, and with a *sharp look-out ahead* a pleasant little coast over the gently sloping road is cautiously indulged in; down, down we spin, following the main road to the right over the well worn surface, and on, on we glide, past the dwellings of the rich and poor, directly through the business section of the settlement, until in a few minutes we reach the " Square," so called, at the village center. Passing the pump at this place on our left, we continue the ride over the mud-covered highway, enjoying highly the magnificent stretch of harbor scenery before us. A short distance, and the first dismount is now taken at the foot of a rough incline known as " Patch's Hill." At this place are a number of prominent Summer cottages, among them being the Delphine House, Craig Cottage and Brazier Cottage, each affording first-class accommodations, with facilities for bathing, fishing and boating in close proximity. Once again we bestride the slender wheel and continue on for half a dozen rods or more to the gate-way at the entrance to Niles' Beach, which marks the terminus of the public way.

Our trip on the bicycle in this direction has finished, and so we sit awhile on the near-at-hand rocky bluff and watch the merry throng of bathers in their sportive antics in the cooling sea, and inwardly wish that we were among them in the refreshing exercise. At our back, as we sit facing the sandy shore, is the little Summer abode of the well-known authoress, Elizabeth Stuart Phelps—the cottage in which she has already penned a number of interesting works, and where she passes the greater portion of the long, warm Summer days. Directly in front of us, at the further end of the beach, is the old mansion house of the Niles family, and still further on, at the extreme end of the rocky shore, is the tall stone column of Eastern Point Light.

The walk across the beach and over the narrow winding tree-bordered path is well worth taking, and makes a pleasant ramble for the visiting tourist. At the lighthouse the visitor should certainly pass a few moments—the tower is well worth careful inspection ; and the fishing, with long bamboo poles, from the rocks in this vicinity, affords considerable sport, being generally attended with satisfactory results. The old fort on the left, as you proceed along toward the Point, should not be missed—you enjoy a pleasant half hour by just sitting on the ruined parapet and gazing out over the bosom of the grand old sea. These fortifications were erected during the "late unpleasantness," mounted ten mammoth guns, and at one time was a military post of considerable importance, commanding as it did the entrance to our harbor and a wide range of the adjacent bay. I believe, though, no occasion demanded its active services during the entire season of its occupancy. "Niles' Pond," a beautiful lake of fresh water covering nearly thirty acres, will also be noticed in this vicinity.

Returning from the pleasant walk around the Niles property, we again secure our position on the pear-shaped seat, and once more resume our ride, this time following along the Point road, over which we recently came, for perhaps a quarter mile, then turning up the long incline leading to Mount Pleasant avenue at the right, near the entrance to which stand the two large icehouses of Mr. Patch, we continue the trip over a fairly good surface and through a particularly interesting section of the town. On we go, flitting by the dwelling houses and green fields at a lively canter, passing the cemetery on our left, and finally reach a more open country. Now we drink eagerly of the deliciously cool sea breeze that comes over the farm lands from the deep blue waters around us, and for the first time notice, with a keen sense of enjoyment, the beautiful panoramic picture spread out before our eyes. We are loth to leave the vicinity, so impressed are we with the magnificent stretch of land and ocean scenery ;

Pass Rock House, F. H. Nunns, Proprietor.

and while seriously contemplating a dismount to more fully enjoy the beauties of the place, a turn in the road now brings us into the avenue leading to the famous seashore resort known as the "Bass Rock" settlement.

The Bass Rock House looms up before us almost directly after entering the thoroughfare, and the pleasing little coast we now take brings us directly to the hotel door. This hotel at Bass Rocks has recently been appointed by consul Burnham of Gloucester a league headquarters, and wheelmen will be cordially entertained at any time during the Summer. The house is one of the finest on the coast, being noted particularly for the excellence of its cuisine. Special rates to L. A. W. tourists.

You catch a good idea of this charmingly situated seaside settlement in a ride along the road leading on past the hotel grounds toward the rocky coast below. The land hereabouts was originally owned in "cow rights" by different parties, and was long known by the name of "Harbor Pasture." About the year 1846 Mr. George H. Rogers, then a prominent merchant of Gloucester, began the purchase of these "cow rights" and soon acquired possession of the entire territory comprising them. Mr. Rogers, it is believed, foresaw the advantages this beautiful tract of land offered as a future seashore resort, and at once began the improvement of the property by laying out avenues and roadways, cutting up the pasture into suitable building lots and otherwise greatly enhancing the value of the premises, expending vast sums of money in the work. Mr. Rogers died, however, before he realized any pecuniary benefit from the outlay, and the property was sold to Mr. Henry Souther, of South Boston, Mass., who in turn sold it to the Gloucester Land Company. This Company built a small hotel, sold several of the building lots, and then the property passed again into the hands of Mr. Souther, who is the present owner. This gentleman immediately began the work of bringing the property into market, and spent considerable money in further improving it; a'large addition was built to the small hotel, cottages were erected, new driveways constructed and the old ones rebuilt, and soon the section became noted as one of the most attractive on the coast.

Among the many private residences here is that of Attorney-General Edgar J. Sherman, of Lawrence, whose house stands directly upon the rocky cliff overhanging Bass Rock itself, to which the building is securely bolted. The scene from the spacious veranda of this dwelling is a grand one—to the left is noticed the long white sandy strip of Little Good Harbor beach; on our right the noble old ocean stretches out in its grandeur to the sky; Salt island and Thacher's lie directly in front of us, the two tall lighthouses on the latter rising like grim sentinels above the vasty deep; while seventy odd feet beneath us the "sad sea waves" dash with terrific force against the huge jagged rocks, sending a thick blanket of snow-white foam afar out over the restless surface of the little cove.

To see Bass Rocks in its glory one must visit the place during a storm; then the waters roll up in mountainous waves, and breaking against the rocky shore send thousands of tons of spray completely over the dwelling on the cliff above.

Another hotel, the Pebbly Beach House, stood at the extreme end of the shore road, and was quite a favorite establishment with the Summer tourist. This building was burned to the ground during the Spring of last year.

In returning from this section of the town we begin the journey at the Bass Rock Hotel, upon the road leading off at a right angle with the one over which we recently wheeled, and soon reach the descending slope of the curving way. Wheelmen should *keep a sharp outlook* from this point, for the meeting with a coming team or striking one of the numberless pieces of loose granite on the rough surface of the road might cause a serious accident to the rider and wheel. Once around the curve, our feet are taken from the pedals and down the gravelly descent we rapidly coast, enjoying the beautiful scenery on the right. The turn in the road ahead is cautiously taken and we are soon at the bottom and safely wheeling over the narrow pathway by the side of Bass Rock avenue. Then the familiar East Main street, at the "head of the harbor," is taken, and over this thoroughfare we rapidly wheel, and soon arrive at the Gloucester Hotel.

This trip to Eastern Point is one affording much enjoyment, and if his time will allow, the visiting bicyclist should not fail to take it in.

II—SAUNTERINGS AT MAGNOLIA.

One of the most attractive sections of Cape Ann is the bit of seashore property in the extreme southwest corner of the territory, known as Magnolia, a section which a few years ago was but a small fishing hamlet, now widely known as one of the leading fashionable Summer resorts along the northeast coast.

A bicycle trip to this picturesque settlement from Gloucester proper is one especially recommended to visiting wheelmen, as much of interest is to be seen in the ride over the four-mile route and in and around the famous little village on the rock-bound shore.

The start begins with the wheelman at the league hotel, and is first along the familiar Western avenue, over the bridge, to the buildings of Cressy at the extreme end of the "Cut road," so called; thence on up the long gravelly incline of Bray's hill, from the top of which a most enjoyable picture greets our eye, including the harbor of Gloucester, and an extensive range of the bay beyond. Now the pace is quickened, and with "legs over," the hill in front of us is rapidly coasted to the foot.

From this point on, the surface of the road is covered with a thick layer of loose gravel, which, in connection with the several short steep inclines, makes the ride a trifle difficult for the bicyclist. With due exercise of care, however, the hills are all easily mounted, and the sandy surface, I am sure, will not particularly annoy the practiced wheelman.

The route now follows along the rocky shore; at our right looms up a massive tree covered cliff, on which stands the Summer residence of the Dale family; at our left, as we round the curving road, can be seen the breaking waves of the sea seventy odd feet below, as they dash up against the rock-bound coast. Soon we pass the elegant Summer home of Mr. Henry S. Hovey, a large finely built mansion in the Swiss style of architecture, standing quietly in the midst of the thick shadow of the woods; and just beyond, at the foot of the hill, is the prettily situated English villa at Brookbank, belonging to Samuel E. Sawyer, Esq., a Summer resident, who recently donated the beautiful library building to his native town.

At Sawyer's hill I would advise the wheelman to dismount from his machine, as the road here is badly cut up and likely to cause the rider a severe "header." If the hill must be ridden, let the wheelman take the "coast" at the top, with a firm hold upon the brake and a watchful eye on the curve ahead.

Once over the hill, the rider continues along the county highway with its fairly good surface of well trodden gravel, and soon the wheelman reaches a section of the route leading directly through the thick woods. The "Troy" house is quickly reached and passed, then the tree-bordered road brings us to the narrow causeway with its well hardened surface, over which we rapidly pedal and where, for the first time, we begin to really enjoy the beauties of the trip. The descending slope of Bennett's hill now appears in front of us, and down the smooth surface we spin with "legs over handles"—a charming little coast, by the way, that carries us nearly around the curve in the road ahead. We now find the way more level, and it requires but a few minutes' ride ere we reach the sign-board on the left of the road that points out the way to the settlement on Magnolia Point.

The ride over this Magnolia avenue, as it is called, is particularly enjoyable. You catch a pleasing view of the little seaside village, with its attractive surroundings, and are not at all surprised at its boasted popularity as a Summer resort. The long gracefully curved Crescent beach lies off at our right, with its white sandy surface sloping gradually to the finely formed cove in front; at our left loom up the densely wooded hills; and as we proceed along the way we note the many beautiful private dwellings, hotels and boarding houses that go to make the settlement.

Since attention was first attracted to it Magnolia has grown rapidly as a seaside resort. Scarce a dozen years ago the entire section hereabouts was covered with a thick growth of underbrush—no house stood upon the territory excepting the rough shanties of the fishermen down by the shore; now the place is laid out in fine style—roads of from forty to fifty feet in width run from the main highway up towards the neighboring woods, and turning, lead down to the rock-bound shore and follow along its very edge.

The work of laying out the settlement was begun by the late Daniel W. Fuller, of Swampscott, in the year 1867, and to that gentleman is the present prosperity of the Point section justly credited. Mr. Fuller with great taste cut up the property into suitable building lots, with convenient roadways connecting them. On several of the lots this pioneer erected trim-looking cottages, which found ready purchasers, and in 1877 built the hotel on Hesperus avenue, where it now stands. The hotel was enlarged during the spring of 1879 by the addition of a large "wing" on the eastern side, connected to the main house by a covered walk sixty feet in length. This house is among the best in the vicinity for visiting tourists—nearly every room in the building commands a most magnificent view of the bay and ocean. Other hotels at Magnolia are: Willow Cottage, on the main avenue, situated beneath the spreading branches of the mammoth trees that give to it its name; Ocean-Side, on Lexington avenue, a charmingly situated edifice, with extensive piazzas, from which a wide range of ocean scenery is obtained; Oak Grove House, on a way leading off from the main avenue and within the shelter of a thick grove of oaks; the Crescent Beach Hotel, the tall two and-a-half-story French roof building noticed away off on the right as we ride over the road leading to the Point, which stands just over the Magnolia line, and was built some few years ago by Mr. Allen Knowlton. The wheelman will have no occasion to find fault with any hotel at Magnolia—all are first-class in every particular and well worthy the liberal patronage they each enjoy.

Among the many notable private residences at Magnolia Point are those of Rev. H. W. Foote (of King's Chapel, Boston); Mr. James Perkins; J. G. Aborn; Alice D. Goodwin; Mr. Trowbridge; the "Upland Cottage" on Flume road; Col. C. G. Thornton; Charles A. Cummings; Dr. F. G. Morrill; and others.

Many pleasant walks and rambles radiate from Magnolia. The dense woods back of the shore are threaded by innumerable carriage and foot paths, that offer unusual attractions to the stroller. The wheelman should certainly enjoy the walk over the old path leading from Flume road and skirting the rocky shore: the sight-seer soon reaches the "Flume," a channel in the cliff over one hundred and fifty feet in length by forty odd in width, with sides almost perpendicular in their descent. Just beyond is another natural gap, or ravine, in the high mainland cliff, into which at every tide the waters of the bay roll with a force most terrific.

"Rafe's Chasm," also in the near vicinity, is still another remarkable illustration of the wonderful works of Dame Nature. Here is a deeply cut fissure in the solid ledge, extending from the sea inland a couple of hundred feet, by sixty feet in depth, with a width ranging from three to fifteen feet. At all times the sea rushes with tremendous force into this rock-bound channel, churning the water into a milk-white foam and sending the spray in torrents over the bluffs adjacent. Just after a storm is the best time to visit Rafe's Chasm—then the visitor becomes more forcibly impressed with the wondrous power of the mighty sea, for the "mad unchained elements" surge with such violence into the cavernous opening as to produce a noise, loud and continual, akin almost to the thunder of the heavens. The iron cross on the cliff at this point was erected by the Summer people of Magnolia in memory of Miss Martha Marvin of Walton, N. Y., who was swept off the rocks below by the treacherous sea during the summer of 1879.

Following the old path again, the rambler soon espies the famous reef of "Norman's Woe," a small island of solid rock situated a few hundred yards from the main land. This rock, tradition tells, was the scene of the wreck of the schooner "Hesperus," the latter part of the seventeenth century, which has been immortalized in verse by the poet Longfellow:

> "It was the schooner Hesperus,
>   That sailed the wintry sea;
> And the skipper had taken his little daughter
>   To bear him company.
> *   *   *   *   *   *   *

IN AND AROUND CAPE ANN.

Colder and louder blew the wind,
    A gale from the northeast;
The snow fell hissing in the brine,
    And the billows frothed like yeast.

*   *   *   *   *   *   *

Down came the storm, and smote amain
    The vessel in its strength;
She shuddered and paused like a frighted steed,
    Then leaped her cable's length.

*   *   *   *   *   *   *

'O father! I see a gleaming light;
    Oh, say, what may it be?'
But the father answered never a word,
    A frozen corpse was he.

Lashed to the helm, all stiff and stark,
    With his face turned to the skies,
The lantern gleamed through the gleaming snow
    On his fixed and glassy eyes.

And fast through the midnight dark and drear,
    Through the whistling sleet and snow,
Like a sheeted ghost the vessel swept
    Towards the reef of Norman's Woe.

The breakers were right beneath the bows,
    She drifted a dreary wreck,
And a whooping billow swept the crew
    Like icicles from her deck.

She struck where the white and fleecy waves
    Looked soft as carded wool,
But the cruel rocks, they gored her side
    Like the horns of an angry bull.

*   *   *   *   *   *   *

At day-break, on the bleak sea-beach,
    A fisherman stood aghast
To see the form of a maiden fair
    Lashed close to a drifting mast.

> The salt sea was frozen on her breast;
>   The salt tears in her eyes;
> And he saw her hair, like the brown sea-weed,
>   On the billows fall and rise.
>
> Such was the wreck of the Hesperus
>   In the midnight and the snow!
> Christ save us all from a death like this,
>   On the reef of Norman's Woe!"

The walk along the old path by the rocky shore is, perhaps, the most attractive ramble in the vicinity of Magnolia. This section of seashore property has recently come into the possession of the Magnolia Shore Association, which company will no doubt soon place the same upon the market, in suitable building lots for the summer resident.

The view of the ocean is a most extensive one from any point along this shore; we have but to stretch forth our hand and grasp the lighthouse on Eastern Point, it seems so near at hand. Massachusetts bay makes a pretty picture to look upon, with the white-winged craft decorating its tossing surface, and far across the waters can be seen the dull blue headlands of Cape Cod, rising cloud-like from that sandy shore.

Back of the rocky shore the rambler finds the same uneven and irregular surface, though covered with a thick growth of native trees, among which

> "..... maples spread their cooling shade
> and tall oaks kiss the sky."

Berries of nearly every kind are here found in great abundance, and also that sweetest of all the wild flowers of early spring, the "trailing arbutus." In the great tree-covered swamp beyond these hills thrives the famous "Magnolia" or sweet bay shrub, growing from ten to a dozen feet in height, with a beautiful smooth green foliage and large white, sweet-scented flowers, first discovered by a Dr. Cutler, and which is found in no other spot on the territory of the New England states. It is this flower that suggested the name for the attractive summer resort near at hand.

The improvements at Magnolia are yearly adding much to the attractiveness of the settlement; a considerable sum of money was raised among the summer residents at a fair at the Hesperus House, during the last season, for the purpose of erecting a chapel for religious purposes, and the corner-stone of the new edifice was successfully laid on Sunday, August 24, 1884, with appropriate services, on the lot on Fuller street between the Fuller cottage and the residence of Mr. Piper. The new building will be known as "Union Chapel," and is not to be used by any one denomination or sect exclusively.

A new piece of road connecting Magnolia Point with the main highway has recently been built, by order of the County Commissioners, from a point on Magnolia avenue opposite Norman avenue, which now shortens the distance from the settlement to the railroad station at least a mile.

A society known as the Magnolia Improvement Society has recently been formed for the purpose, as its name implies, of protecting and developing the natural and social attractions of the place and the general improvement of the standard and tone of the village life.

The wheelman will greatly enjoy a day or two at this seaside resort; if he wishes a pleasant sail upon the waters of the adjoining bay, he has but to seek the owner of one of the numerous craft anchored within the neighboring cove. Fishing is prime sport, and may be indulged in from off the rocks or in the deep sea farther out. Bathing is excellent on the half-mile crescent-shaped beach, and one will have no cause for complaint at the absence of any of the popular attractions common to the fashionable summer resort of the period.

In returning to Gloucester the wheelman will find a pleasant trip via "Little River Road," so called, to West Gloucester, thence to Essex avenue, and so on to the city proper.

III—BY WHEEL TO CHEBACCO POND.

Another enjoyable ride for the 'cyclist, for a short run, is the twelve-mile trip to Hamilton and the Chebacco Lakes. This route has especial attractions for the wheelman, lying as it does through a country of farm-lands and meadows of much picturesque beauty. There is but a single unrideable hill in the entire course, and the run is easily made in one and a quarter hours. Gloucester riders consider this trip one of the most pleasant wheel runs in the vicinity.

From the league hotel the way is over Western avenue to the road turning off toward the right and leading over the marsh, just after passing the bridge, thence the route follows along Essex avenue, as the way is called, up the short incline of Lovett's hill, and on, over a new piece of road-way, for about a mile and a half, then the neat and trim-looking stable of the Fernwood Lake Ice Co. comes into view on the left of the road, and here the wheelman may dismount, if he so chooses, for a cooling drink at the stone basin near at hand. The newly-built roadway at this point leads to the lake itself, situated a few hundred feet only from the main highway; this lake, the property of Mr. F. W. Homans, furnishes a large proportion of the ice used by the Gloucester fishing vessels, besides keeping supplied a considerable retail business during the summer. The mammoth house here measures 210 by 237 feet, and is the largest in the state; it has a storage capacity of 40,000 tons.

From Fernwood lake to the city proper the road is sadly out of repair, due, in a great measure, to the heavy teaming of the ice company, which is almost constant over it; the surface is generally covered with a layer of muddy gravel from four to eight inches deep, and gullies and ruts across the way about every ten feet of the distance; the road is rideable, however, if the wheelman uses a little extra care and does not attempt a "flying" pace. A few hundred yards beyond the Fernwood stables, and the rider reaches the long, gradual descent known as Railroad hill, situated in West Gloucester, and within a few rods of the Boston & Maine railroad. In descending this hill much caution should be exercised, for the road is rough, and that curve at the foot may hide some approaching team; for this reason the coast, if taken at all, should not commence until the wheelman reaches that point from which he can view the remainder of the way, then, with "legs over," the descent can be finished with safety.

And now begins the better portion of the trip; from this point on, the wheelman finds the road surface in good condition for his rubber-tired wheel, and it is with thorough enjoyment that he notes the beautiful stretch of scenery constantly before his eye; the farm-lands and houses flit by him in rapid succession; the country church and wayside store, with the village post office, come into view and are as quickly left behind; woodlands and meadows abound on either hand, and now and then the dark blue waters of the Annisquam river rise before him in the distance, forming in the whole a grand picture of unsurpassing beauty and well worth the trip to see.

Henry C. L. Haskell, Esq., is a good authority on matters of particular interest to the tourist, at West Gloucester; he can be found at the post office, and will cheerfully render any assistance in his power to all members of the wheeling fraternity. Mount Thompson, at this place, should be visited by the sightseer; a magnificent view is obtained from its summit.

A short distance from the West Gloucester post office and the wheelman reaches "Slough hill," a narrow portion of the road hemmed in by massive ledges of rough granite. This hill has a discouraging look in the eye of the 'cyclist, as he views the incline from the farther end of the level approach, but he will experience no difficulty in riding to the top if he is careful to avoid the many gullies of loose sand that dot the road surface at this point.

Beyond Slough hill the road continues its winding course, rising and falling in graceful swells like the bosom of old ocean; huge trees border the way on either hand, and occasionally the pretty farm-house shows itself in a cleared place by the roadside. The wheelman now takes advantage of the sand-papered country highway, and on he speeds in his noiseless ride for perhaps ten minutes; then he reaches a slight rise in the road surface, from which a good view is had of the town of Essex just beyond; now do a little rapid work on the pedals and you catch a pleasing coast, that should carry you around the curve to the sign-board on the right of the way, which sign-board is just five and a half miles from the Gloucester Hotel.

Now turning to the left, the ride continues over the narrow road across the marsh, and on into the busy little country town of Essex. Following the road directly through the settlement the 'cyclist quickly reaches the long causeway with its many ship-yards, where for a few minutes we will take a brief halt for a look around the place. The town of Essex, as almost every one knows, is noted particularly for its ship-building. This business has gained for the little village a justly entitled prominence, second to none other in the country, for here are built some of the staunchest craft that floats the waters; nearly all of the Gloucester fleet were launched at Essex, and certain it is, that no better vessels than those that stand the terrific gales of Georges and the Western Banks float upon the sea to-day. These vessels are all of the clipper type, with graceful lines and thoroughly built. Among the largest builders here are A. D. Story and Moses Adams; the former built and launched during the year just closed, 13 vessels, aggregating nearly 1030 tons and valued at $100,000 when ready for sea. Mr. Adams did a business of over $60,000 during the same season. Last spring (1884) the firm of John James & Co. launched the largest vessel built in Essex—the three-masted schooner "Julia Fowler," owned by W. H. Ryder and others of Boston. This craft, which was built for the coast trade, had a white oak frame and planking, and hard pine ceiling; her dimensions were 300 tons (carpenter's measurement), 213 net tonnage, length 120 feet over all, beam 27 feet, hold 11 feet, draught 12 feet, value, all ready for sea, $20,000. The best prices contractors received were $65 and $70 per ton, which was during the war period; last year the price averaged about $45 per ton. Ship carpenters earn on an average $2.50 per day, and good calkers from $18 to $20 per week during the busy season. The best profits, contractors find in the fishing vessels of 75 to 100 tons, and they are better prepared to build them than any other class; the building of large vessels has long ago gone farther to the eastward; the last large one built here was in 1840—a 400-ton ship. Ten years ago the James firm did quite a business in three-masted schooners, but this, too, has dropped off considerably since.

Essex originally formed a part of Ipswich, and was long known

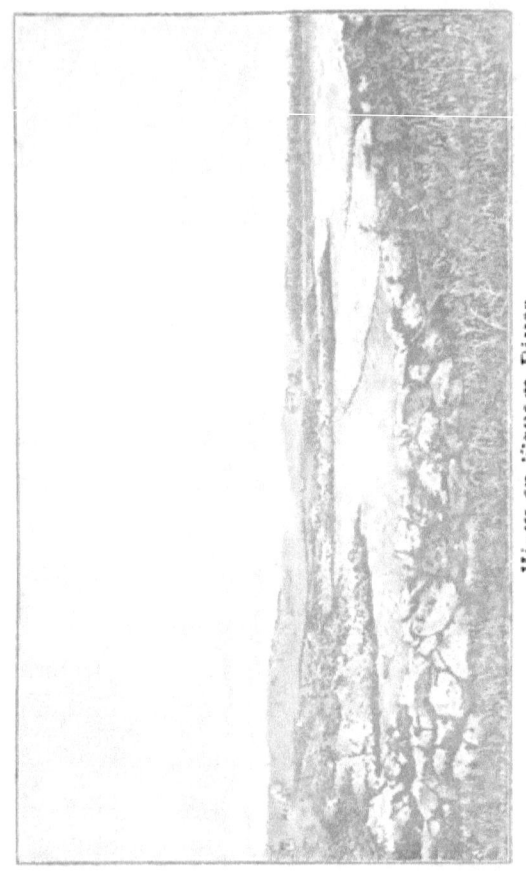

View on 'Squam River.

as "Chebacco"; it was incorporated a town in 1819; situated in the easterly part of the county of Essex, it is bounded northerly by Ipswich, easterly by Gloucester, southerly by Manchester, and westerly by the town of Hamilton, from which it is separated for a considerable distance by the Chebacco Pond. It was at Essex that the first craft was built that afterward were so common on the north-east coast as "Chebacco boats"; it is said that the builder did the work upon the new craft in an upper story of his dwelling house, and that when the boat was finished it was found necessary to take away the window frames and nearly the entire side of the building in order to get the affair out for launching.

From Chebacco Pond flows the Essex river, a small stream emptying into the sea at a point between Castle Neck in Ipswich and Two Penny Loaf in Gloucester; this stream divides the settlement into two nearly equal sections. "Hog Island," a rounded knoll containing several fine farms, is situated between Castle Neck and the main land, and is noted especially as the birthplace of the eminent lawyer and statesman, Rufus Choate, in the year 1799. In the near vicinity of Hog island is Cross' island, on which is the Summer residence of H. A. Burnham, Jr.—the L. A. W. consul of Gloucester—where wheelmen may be sure of a cordial reception whenever they chance to happen in the near vicinity.

The people of Essex are industrious and hospitable. Besides ship-building, farming, gardening and fishing are carried on somewhat extensively; boots and shoes are also manufactured; and since the opening of the Essex Branch of the Eastern railroad a considerable ice business has continued, the Chebacco Pond furnishing an excellent quality for transportation.

Leaving the shipyards at Essex, the wheelman continues the

ride up the short hill past the meeting-house and down the road leading off toward the left, pointed out by the sign-board here as the way to Hamilton. The road going toward the right will take one to Ipswich and Newburyport, and is usually in a fine condition for bicycle riding.

Essex soon drops behind the 'cyclist, for before him the way opens with that good hard surface so common to the country roads in the vicinity, and up and down the gently rising grades, following the narrow winding way, flitting on past the many well-kept farms and orchards, does the happy wheelman spin. A guide-board soon again points out the right direction, and then the way continues up a long easily ridable incline and on around a gigantic curve that admits of an enjoyable view of the pleasing farm-land country; soon another guide-board appears at the entrance to the famous Centennial Grove, and at this point the rider gets his first view of the deep blue surface of the Chebacco Lakes; now the road surface is more broken—sharp-pointed stones dot the heretofore sand-papered way, and an inch or two of finely powdered sand, a little further on, makes it necessary for careful riding; the hill beneath the willows is a treacherous one for 'cycling on account of a deep gravelly surface—it is a short one, though, and ridable for the rubber-tired wheel. At the top again the wheelman finds himself on a pleasing level, and now he casts his eye with delight at the beautiful panoramic picture before him; just look to the right and notice those mammoth hills rearing their green covered tops well up into the sky —it seems as though some wonderful freak of nature had caused this gigantic tumbling and shaking up of the surface of mother Earth just to test the effect of its unrivalled powers, so grandly impressive is the picture.

A few yards farther on and the first dismount becomes a

necessity, for the road now leads up that broad, sweeping hill on the left with a surface of from three to six inches of sandy gravel nearly to its summit. I never saw this hill in condition for the bicyclist to climb. The one particular spot that annoys the rider is on the level at the foot of the incline; here the sandy surface always measures from six to ten inches in depth, through which it is almost impossible to propel the rubber-rimmed machine. At the top another grand view is obtained of the surrounding country, and it is a picture always recalled to the mind of the beholder.

Mounting the wheel again, the rider continues the way along a narrow tree-bordered road with a fairly good surface, and soon reaches the crossing of the Essex branch of the Boston & Maine railroad. The station to the right, at this point, is known as "Woodbury's Crossing," where the wheelman may take the train for Salem or beyond, if he feels so disposed. A few minutes' ride from this point and the trip nears its end, for at the first road turning off at the left the wheelman will notice a sign-board that points the way to the "Chebacco House and the Lakes." Into this the way continues, and now the 'cyclist catches a most delightful spin over the well-hardened track; how the thick woods on our right seem to fly past us as we proceed along, and how deliciously cool does the sweetly scented breeze come to us as we rapidly coast that gently falling grade adown the wooded road; on we glide with "legs over," around the projecting point of the lake waters and up the little rise ahead, then again with "legs over" do we take advantage of the sand-papered slope before us, and so we reach "Whipple's," our face a trifle flushed with the excitement of the last half-mile spurt. Here our machine is given into the hands of the genial 'Lonzo—who, by the way, is a warm friend of the wheeling fraternity—and then after a wash up at the hotel beyond, we are ready for the stroll around on foot.

I suppose almost everybody has heard more or less of Chebacco Pond and the famous hotel at this place kept by Messrs. A. L. & S. A. F. Whipple, and of the broiled chicken dinners of those caterers, that long ago made the reputation of the house —a reputation held strong to-day, it being the one great drawing card of the establishment. Day after day, through the long Summer months, on Sundays especially, are the dining rooms of this hostlery well filled with happy hungry beings, whose merry prattle and joyous laughter make the old walls fairly ring as the toothsome viands are being disposed of. Wheelmen are cordially welcomed at this hotel, as any and every thing will be done for them by the painstaking management.

The rambles around the Chebacco lakes are many, and afford much enjoyment to the sight-seer. You walk down to the large pond, and much of interest presents itself. Afar off on the further side of the lake, as you sit upon the structure built into the water at this point, is noticed the buildings at Centennial Grove, the camp-ground of the Salem Cadets for the past two seasons. The lad will furnish you with sail or row boat for a pleasing sail upon the deep blue surface, or for fishing, as one feels disposed ; perch, pickerel and trout abound in these lakes, and considerable sport is thus open to the visitor. The way leading through the woods to Manchester is a particularly romantic walk for the rambling tourist ; on this road, which is ridable for the wheelman a considerable portion of the way, will be noticed the placid, glass-like surface of "Gravel Pond," a sheet of water almost shut in entirely from its outside surroundings by several high tree-covered hills.

The Indian name of Chebacco means " Place of Spirits,"

though why it should thus be called is not the purport of this article to explain. The lake, covering nearly two hundred and sixty acres, is mostly within the limits of the town of Hamilton.

Other points of interest in the vicinity will be cheerfully shown the visitor by the proprietors of the Chebacco House, and all should be seen to be fully appreciated.

IV—A WHEEL AROUND CAPE ANN.

If the wheelman would see the most characteristic features of Cape Ann, the trip around the shore road should not be omitted. The route is the most enjoyable of any wheel-run in the vicinity, and leads through a rural district of constantly changing scenery—a country of woods, hills, massive ledges and loose gigantic bowlders, with a grandly impressive picture of ocean scenery for nearly the entire sixteen miles.

The start is made as before, at the Gloucester Hotel, and the ride is first along Main street over the route described in a former chapter as the way to Eastern Point, to the junction of East Main street with Eastern avenue, thence up the latter named thoroughfare to the main county highway leading to the town of Rockport. The road surface begins to improve from this point, and the wheelman rapidly pedals over the narrow side path and soon gets away entirely from the vicinity of the scattered dwelling houses that frequent the locality.

Passing Webster's ice-houses on the left, the tourist continues the route up and down the many gradual rises, through the patches of newly-laid road material, and on, over the pleasing smooth portions of the country road until the short and rough descent is reached near the ice pond of Mr. Day. Beyond this pond the road continues its winding course, and then the rider reaches a more open section of country. Now the first of a series of most enjoyable pictures presents itself to the eye of the beholder: Away off to the right is seen a long white stretch of sandy beach, with the ocean and islands beyond and the attractive Bass Rock settlement at East Gloucester; back of us, and to our left, rise great rugged-looking hills and mammoth ledges; while all around us, on either hand, are countless numbers of loosely lying bowlders of almost every conceivable shape and size.

We now speed upon a newly-built piece of road at this point, extending around a massive hill of rock, and soon pass the picturesque-looking residence of the Hon. John J. Babson, the historian of Gloucester, amid the waving branches of the thickly growing trees at our right; just beyond, a guide-board flits by us with its "Rockport, 2½ miles," then with a flying spurt we easily climb the little hill ahead and soon come to a tree-bordered section of the route.

The roadway for the next mile is generally in a poor condition for bicycle riding, though with care the greater portion of that distance may be gotten over without a dismount from the machine; the pace, however, must be a slow one, for the sandy surface hides innumerable sharply pointed stones and loose pebbles, that are sure to cause the rider a serious mishap if he without warning attempts to ride rapidly over them.

We cross the boundary line between Gloucester and Rockport in this vicinity, and in a few minutes reach Beaver Dam Farm on the left-hand side, with its quaint looking stone structure bearing the inscription, "Beaver Dam, 1832," reminding one most forcibly of an oasis amid the surrounding country of hills and ledges. Opposite Beaver Dam, snugly nestling within the deep shadows of the high forest-covered hills, lies the famous sheet of fresh water known as Cape Pond, with a beautiful grove for picnic parties upon its shores.

Soon after passing Beaver Dam the rider follows along the route, side by side with the railroad track, and then reaches a portion of the trip that will test his abilities to the utmost as a hill climber. Great Hill looms before the wheelman for quite a distance ere the base is reached, and its good hard-looking surface tempts the 'cyclist to the task he afterward gladly resigns, for the incline is a long one and well calculated to give the veteran wheelman a severe trial ; to the inexperienced road rider the hill is unridable, and such tourists should avoid taxing their strength by dismounting at the end of the rail fence on the left side of the road. This hill is a grand one for coasting, on the return, though the machine should be kept well under control at the start. From the top of Great Hill, as the 'cyclist wheels along, the picture is truly grand : Away ahead the spires and steeples of Pigeon Cove and Rockport sparkle brightly under the glare of the burning sun ; off to the right is a long blue stretch of ocean surface and the famous Thacher's island with its two tall lighthouses that seem to guard like sentinels Cape Ann's rock-bound coast ; behind us fields, woodlands and lofty hills are noticed, with a far-off view of the ice-houses at Fernwood lake in West Gloucester. All in all, the picture is the most pleasing from this standpoint than from any other upon the Cape, including, as it does, the greater portion of the prominent features that characterize the headland of Cape Ann.

And now the gradual slope into the town of Rockport begins, and away speeds the rambling 'cyclist directly into the village center, following the main thoroughfare, then turning into Railroad avenue, continuing on up the short incline and passing the station on the left to North street, down the long gently sloping

Pigeon Cove House, Mrs. E. S. Robinson & Co., Proprietors.

surface of which we rapidly spin with legs over handles, once again meeting the county highway, and soon reaching the stone bridge of the Rockport Granite Company.

Upon entering the town of Rockport the stranger at once notices the many uses to which the chief product of the locality is put—stone houses, stone churches, stone fences, stone piers—it is stone, stone everywhere. Mammoth ledges of handsome looking granite confront the sight-seer on every hand; these ledges once covered the entire territory hereabouts for many miles around, but long years of constant clipping upon them have produced a wondrous change in the original condition of the land—little by little have the deep gullies and basins been extended into the solid rock, until it now seems as though, indeed, the very bowels of the earth must be exposed.

The view from this stone bridge to the eastward is particularly enjoyable, as, indeed, it is for the remainder of the trip to Pigeon Cove. The cyclometer should here register $5\frac{1}{8}$ miles, and at the long hill beyond, at Pigeon Cove, $6\frac{1}{2}$ miles. The surface of the road from the bridge, for the balance of the trip around the Cape, is simply magnificent for the rubber-tired wheel, and fully repays the 'cyclist for the little extra work attending the run from Gloucester to this point.

The hill at Pigeon Cove is easily ridden by the wheelman—take the left side going up—and at the pleasant and cosy looking Pigeon Cove House, at the top, we will dismount for a brief ramble around the locality.

Pigeon Cove has long held a prominent position among the popular Summer resorts of the northeast coast, having as it does its own especial attractions for the rambling Summer tourists. The earliest Summer visitor to this vicinity was Richard H. Dana, Sr., who came in 1840 in search of a pleasant seaside retreat; he was greatly pleased with the locality, and for a number of years afterward spent many delightful seasons here in company with his friend, William Cullen Bryant. These gentlemen, though both somewhat reserved and retiring in manner, sought out and visited the homes of the villagers, and conversed pleasantly with the inmates of the many abodes sequestered in the woods, and in the little fishing shanties along the rocky shore —words that to-day are still recalled and repeated with mingled pride and pleasure. Mr. Bryant, after purchasing his Summer house on Long Island, did not again visit the vicinity of Pigeon Cove, and Mr. Dana finally built an elegant residence at Manchester, Mass., on the south shore of the Cape.

Pigeon Cove is the North Village of Rockport. The uneven surface of the territory is covered with great shaggy looking hills of granite, interspersed with quiet valleys and overrun with thousands of narrow winding foot-paths and shady lanes. Its bold rock-bound shore indented with numerous little coves and inlets, makes the chances easy and good for either boating, bathing or fishing. The Pigeon Cove House, at which the wheelman is now resting, is the best in the locality; its proprietress, Mrs. E. S. Robinson, is devoted to the work of catering to the wants of seashore visitors, and is sure to please her patrons; wheelmen are especially recommended to this house—a slight discount from regular rates will be allowed them. The Ocean View, just back of the Pigeon Cove House, is also a good hotel for the tourist; the building commands a grand view of the broad Atlantic.

Back of the hotels and bordering on the rocky shore, is the famous section laid out by Messrs. Babson and Phillips a few years ago. This section, comprising some fifty odd acres, is upon the extreme end of Cape Ann, and is one of the most desirable locations for the Summer cottager upon the entire New England coast. Finely graded and well kept avenues and walks traverse the territory, crossing and recrossing each other, now at right angles, again in graceful curves, sometimes along the rocky shore, sometimes through groves of pines and oaks, and winding through an open section, fragrant with the scent of ferns, bayberry shrubs and wild roses—a highly enjoyable trip for the visiting wheelman. Many handsome looking private residences adorn this section, among which may be mentioned those of Mrs. Bishop on Haven avenue, Miss Sara Jewett (the well known leading lady of the Union Square Theatre), Mr. Frothingham, Mr. Thompson, Mr. Willey, Mrs. Chapin of New York, and others on Phillips avenue. The Linwood is the name of the hotel here; it stands upon a high cliff within a couple of hundred feet of the shore; the view from this point is truly magnificent—you see the entire coast to Rockport village, and 'way beyond to Thacher's island with its famous twin lights, where

> "Steadfast, serene, immovable, the same
> Year after year, through all the silent night,
> Burns on forevermore that quenchless flame,
> Shines on that inextinguishable light!"

The bare savage looking rocks known as the Salvages, peep above the restless waves of the open sea, in front of us, about three miles from the shore, while to our left stretches out the broad expanse of Ipswich bay, with the highlands of the "down east" coast easily distinguishable.

The walk and rambles near Pigeon Cove are many and particularly worthy of notice. I will quote a few of the most enjoyable, from the work of Rev. H. C. Leonard on Pigeon Cove:

"It is an easy and pleasant walk to the Breakwater. On this

outer wall of Pigeon Cove harbor the near scene of fishermen at the wharves, and of stone-sloops loading with granite to take to Boston and other cities, is entertaining to those who have not often looked upon it, and even to those to whom it has been a long time familiar. Turning about and looking in the opposite direction, the never uninteresting ocean, the always-the-same and yet the ever changing expanse of waves, glorious in the sun and gay with sailing craft of every description, is surveyed admiringly. From the Breakwater the marginal path is followed along the shore to 'Singers' Bluff,' which overlooks the sea but a few hundred yards from the hotels. Thence the walk is continued by the Bath, where the bathers in picturesque costumes are cheerfully plunging into the sea or dancing in the surf; by the Blue Streaks, veins of trap, some a few inches, others several feet through, which cross the granite Cape from north to south; by Chapin's Rock and Gully, the former at low tide half in the water, the latter a great notch cut into the shore of solid granite where it is highest and boldest; by Ocean Bluff, the outermost footing of Andrews' Point, the farthest Cape Ann projection towards England; thence around Hoop Pole Cove to the old cedar; and so by Cedar avenue, Phillips avenue and Ocean avenue—where the Salvages are seen as a brooch on the bosom of the sea—back to the place of setting out. At the going down of the sun many walk the little distance on the old road of the village to Sunset Rock in the Babson pasture. Here the spectacle of the setting sun, and of the colors that slowly fade while the evening's shades are falling, is the more than reward for strolling a few rods. Returning, Strawberry Hill is climbed. Here Straitsmouth and Thacher's lights on the right, and Ipswich and Newburyport lights on the left, are almost equally distinctly seen; and far over the waves the eye catches the gleam, appearing regularly every few minutes, of the Isles of Shoals revolving light. Those who are vigorous enough for the ramble go to Halibut Point, following the shore from Andrews' Point around Hoop Pole Cove, or by the way of the village road and Captain Gott's Lane; or go to Folly Cove, and Folly Point and the Willows, and thence return by Jumper's Lane, and by a footpath through the woods to Edmunds & Lane's quarry, and then by a quarry road leading to the village in the rear of Overlook, the old House, and Edmunds' Hall; or go to the top of Pigeon Hill by the lane ascending from Mr. Eames' house, or through the woods in a footpath on the northern side of this elevation; or go to the wood-sheltered home of the Knutsfords by the carriage way of the old house, and by grass-covered cart-paths and footpaths the rest of the distance; or go to the quarries on the west and on the south side of Pigeon Hill, by quarry roads, in the shade of a young and thrifty forest all the way; or go to the Moving Rock, in the rear of Lanesville; half way to Annisquam through the woods. This curiosity is a boulder of perhaps eighty tons—so poised on a ledge just appearing above the sward that when pushed against by the shoulders of a man, or pressed by a man's weight upon it, first on one side and then on the other, as one would rock a boat, it will perceptibly vibrate. Under extraordinary pressure its oscillations are seen many yards off. . . . Sometimes ramblers who know the highest and purest enjoyment of rambling, spend day after day in the woods, purposely losing themselves in the complexity of intersecting paths to get the surprises here and there of new views of the sea, and of old ones too, frequently not recognized as familiar till the maze of the forest is left behind."

"A city life who can endure,
  When fields are green and skies are blue;

> When flowers are fragrant—air is pure,
> And Nature's face is fresh and new?"

Before leaving the vicinity of Pigeon Cove, I would suggest that bicyclists intending to stop over at Rockport village, put up at the Abbott House, on Main street. Mr. Harry F. Payne, the gentlemanly proprietor, is particularly agreeable to touring wheelmen, and allows a discount of 20 per cent. from regular tariff rates.

Resuming the ride from the Pigeon Cove House, the wheelman now finds the road more uneven and irregular; it is up hill, down hill, and around hill; the surface remains the same, however, and the 'cyclist has no difficulty in easily mounting the many steep inclines. After turning the curve in the road, near the old Babson homestead, a long gradual descent gives the opportunity for a delightful coast, and the tourist then catches a pleasing view of Folly Cove and the adjacent bay.

The way now leads through a quaint little fishing settlement, and soon the wheelman enters the thriving village of Lanesville, after passing through a section of the road arched completely over with the thickly entwined branches of mammoth willows. A dismount at this cosy looking place, and you have the opportunity of partaking of ice cream or soda at the little wayside store here, kept by Mrs. Marchant. Beyond the willows the road rises with a gradual sweep, continues along by the deeply cut quarries of the Lanesville Granite Company, on past the village store and church, and the dwellings of the few inhabitants, and then the drug store of B. Howard Foster comes into view on the right, at which point we will take a momentary rest for a brief look around.

All that tract of country lying between the Rockport boundary line at Folly Cove on the north and Plum Cove on the

Folly Cove.

south is embraced in that section of Gloucester known as Lanesville. The business is quarrying and fishing; the former is carried on extensively by the Lanesville Granite Co., the Bay State Granite Co., and several other enterprising firms. A considerable amount is invested in the fisheries, and quite a number of men and boats are kept actively employed in this industry throughout the entire season. The granite quarries employ nearly four hundred men, the principal work being in foundation stones and paving. The material for the Masonic Hall building in Philadelphia came from Lanesville, and was furnished by Messrs. George Barker & Co.

Once again securing our position astride the slender wheel, we continue the trip over a pleasing surface through the village center; we now have a number of highly enjoyable coasts, all of which are cautiously indulged in, and almost before we are aware of the fact we sight ahead, at the foot of a long and narrow descent, the busy work-sheds of the world-renowned Cape Ann Granite Co., at Bay View. Down the long hill the coast is taken rapidly, and crossing the tracks of the Granite Co.'s railroad, we begin the long pull up the broad white looking road surface of the hill ahead.

Bay View takes in the territory lying between Plum Cove and the Annisquam meeting-house. The little settlement has become widely known all over the civilized land on account of the excellent quality of its granite for building purposes. It is noted, also, as the Summer residence of Gen. B. F. Butler and Col. Jonas H. French, though of late years the former gentleman has not been a steady sojourner here during the warm season. The General's residence is on the hill above the stone-yards on the right; it is built of granite, and from its spacious verandas the view is most magnificent—the broad expanse of

Ipswich bay lies before you with its numerous white-winged craft, and the shores of Newburyport, Portsmouth and a long line of eastern coast are also plainly discernible. Col, French's residence is noticed on the right, just above the hill; it adjoins the Butler premises, yet unlike the General's, the grounds are laid out with exquisite taste and show evidence of careful cultivation. The granite company here employs from four hundred to seven hundred men the year 'round, and own a large tract of territory extending back from the sea and up the hill for over a mile and a half. It was at Bay View that the granite was quarried for the entire Boston postoffice building; the granite work of the Danvers insane asylum was also furnished by the Cape Ann Company, as also that for the West Point military academy, New England Life Insurance Company building in Boston, and all of the largest columns (25 feet high) and bases of the public library building at Philadelphia. The stones for the base of the monument to Gen. Winfield Scott, at Washington, came from this company, and were the largest pieces ever quarried; the size of the platform was 28.2 x 18.5 x 3.2 feet and weighed 150¾ tons; the sub-base was 21.6 x 11 x 4.10 feet and weighed 104 tons; the base was 18 feet long, 7.10 feet wide and 3.10 feet thick and weighed 48½ tons; with two others, the total weight of these mammoth stones was over 400 tons, and the entire lot was taken from a single quarry, known as the "Blood Quarry." The paving blocks turned out by this company since their occupation of the place in 1869, is almost beyond computation—it ranges well up among the millions, certainly. The company recently shipped a mammoth piece of stone work to New Orleans, to be placed in one of the many French cemeteries there.

From a little work entitled "The North Shore," very pleas-

Davis' Neck, from Gen. Butler's Residence.

ingly written by Messrs. Benj. D. Hill and W. S. Nevins, I quote the following concerning the process of stone quarrying at Bay View:

"The soil being cleared from a ledge and an examination having been made to see how the seams run, a steam drill is set to work boring two holes from 10 to 18 feet in depth and 3 inches in width, and 2 inches apart. A half keg of powder is put in these holes and ignited with electricity. The explosion lifts the ledge from seam to seam, usually in a straight line. Sometimes these lifts are of 20,000 tons weight. The blasts do not smash the rock at all; a person is perfectly safe standing a few feet away. The section of the ledge thus broken off is split into smaller sections, to suit various purposes, with small hand drills and wedges. These pieces are taken to the yard by train, there to be worked into whatever shape desired, with hammer and chisel. The work is mainly done from drawings, though sometimes from patterns. The pieces of stone for the various purposes are entirely prepared at the company's yard, so that there is no cutting or trimming when they arrive at their destination; nothing to do but put them in place. Those men who do the drilling and cutting out of stone, and those who chisel out scroll work and smooth and polish various blocks of granite, work by the day. Those who cut out the small blocks, sold mainly for paving, work by the piece. It requires a man of experience to select the ledges to be worked and direct where the holes shall be drilled. He must understand the grain of the ledge and its seams, and know just which way it will split best. A man of long experience will judge correctly ninety-nine times out of a hundred, while a person of no experience will spoil a ledge as often as he will succeed."

From the quarries the way leads on to the meeting-house at Annisquam, where the main road branches to the right and left. To the left the tree-bordered road winds around the base of a mammoth cliff, nearly fifty feet above the surface of Lobster Cove, the glistening waters of which the rider notices through the branches of the thickly growing trees on the right. The long bridge connecting the main road with the settlement at Annisquam next comes into view, over which the wheelman rapidly spins for a brief visit to that picturesque locality. For a more direct route to this settlement the wheelman should take the road turning toward the *right* near the meeting-house before spoken of.

The territory of Annisquam includes that portion lying between the meeting-house on the north and the junction of the old road with the main highway at Finson Wheeler's on the south. The village is located almost entirely on the westerly side of Lobster Cove. It has of late years gained considerable notoriety as a favorite summer resort, and seashore property in the vicinity has in consequence advanced wonderfully in value in the last ten years. The elevation of land known as the Cambridge avenue section is occupied almost entirely by people from that vicinity; many costly and handsome looking houses have been built here, among the most prominent being those of Dr. Isaac Adams, Mr. Wilmot, Mr. Hall, Mr. Bent, Curtis Davis and W. B. Hastings. Dr. Adams has one of the finest estates in New England; large sums of money have been judiciously expended in beautifying this seaside residence, until now the place is second to none as a comfortable and convenient home. The view from Cambridge avenue is a grand one, including the white-capped bay in front and the winding Annisquam river on the left, looking blue, green and amber in the sun's burning rays; the white sandy shore of Coffin's beach across the way, and the sand covered hills in that vicinity are also conspicuously presented to the naked eye. The picturesque cottage noticed on the extreme edge of the mammoth rocky ledge, and within a few feet only from the restless surface of the treacherous sea, is the residence of George J. Marsh, Esq., of Gloucester. The only hotel in the vicinity is the Grand View on Highland avenue, where wheelmen will be well cared for during their sojourn at the village.

Returning from the pleasantly situated settlement at Annisquam, we once more cross the bridge and continue on the main highway toward Gloucester. The road has a very pleasing surface for bicycling; to be sure, the hills appear as frequently as before, though all are easily ridden and without difficulty. At the foot of the first descent we pass on the right the Summer home of Prof. Alpheus Hyatt, of the Boston Society of Natural History; it occupies a pretty position there by the river side. The view the wheelman now obtains as he wheels along the narrow causeway by the old grist-mill is very fine; at the top of the little elevation ahead he catches a charming sight of the 'Squam settlement, the river and its fleet of gaily decked pleasure craft, Coffin's beach and the deep blue surface of the bay beyond.

The grade of the travelled way now begins a long gradual ascent, at the end of which the picturesque section with the arching willow trees is reached, into which the rider glides with delight, wondering what future surprises the trip may have in store for him. On around the curve the route continues, then the way becomes more level, and the wheelman spins along the fairly good surface, quickly reaching the long, steep and rough descent known as the "meeting-house hill." In descending this hill use extra caution and do not attempt to coast; the machine should be kept well under control by back pedalling and by brake power; keep a watchful eye for teams in rounding the curve at the foot, and be sure and take the *right hand side* in going down.

Now we reach Riverdale mills, so called, and wheel across the bridge here, keeping to the left. We begin to pass the farm lands from this point, and find the road surface more uneven—hills present themselves at every dozen rods or so, and the 'cyclist finds the wheeling just a trifle difficult. Soon the great black mass of rocks, known as the Poles, loom before us on the right, opposite to which the road makes a broad, sweeping turn, with an ascending grade that calls into active service the already weary muscles of the wheelman tourist.

The narrow lane-like way leading from the main road off to the right, just after passing the Poles, will take the tourist to the banks of the Annisquam river; it is but a few hundred yards distant, which the 'cyclist can quickly cover with his rubber-tired wheel. The view from the high knoll that forms the river's bank at this point, is particularly enjoyable. Many pretty cottages can be seen from here dotting the islands and banks of the little stream throughout its entire length, making a picture of much interest to the beholder.

From the Poles the grade of the road takes a long gradual descent that admits of a pleasing coast, and then do we spin along the good hard surface; on past the "Meeting House Green," so called, and around the little bend near the old "Ellery House," then up the short incline ahead and onto the sidewalk of the travelled way.

The old "Ellery House," so called, before spoken of, is one of the oldest buildings in Gloucester. It was built in 1704 as a parsonage for the Rev. John White; a few years afterward the

Willow Road, Riverdale.

dwelling came into the possession of James Stevens, who kept a tavern here till 1740, when Capt. William Ellery bought the place and continued it as a house of entertainment for several years; the house is still held in the possession of his descendants, and presents the same external appearance now as it did when first erected. The Selectmen used to meet at this tavern frequently, often transacting most of the town's business here. As appears by the records of the town, these gentlemen used to have a right royal good time; for instance, one finds— "Expense for the Selectmen and Licker at Mr. James Stevens' Tavern, 3£ 18s. 2d." This was in 1740, and the Selectmen on this occasion were Capt. James Davis, Abraham Davis, Jabez Baker, Nathaniel Ellery and Timothy Day. From the Riverdale mills to the "Meeting House Green" was the section where many of Gloucester's most prominent citizens used to live; in those early days it was the best section of the town.

And now the wheelman rapidly gets within the city's limits, for it is but a short distance after crossing the railroad track to the headquarters at the Gloucester Hotel; and thus terminates the ride around Cape Ann—the most interesting to the rambling 'cyclist of any within the vicinity. The route is about sixteen miles, and can be covered in a couple of hours if the wheelman feels so disposed.

V.—COFFIN'S BEACH.

On the northern shore of Cape Ann, situated between the mouth or entrance of the Annisquam river and the rocky hillock known as "Two Penny Loaf," is another attractive section for the rambling tourist. Coffin's Beach—one of the finest of its kind on the entire Massachusetts coast—here stretches out its hard white looking sandy surface for nearly two miles in distance, and slopes away into the waters of Ipswich bay on such a gradual incline that the out-going tide often retreats a distance of over six hundred feet.

To get to Coffin's Beach by the land route the wheelman tourist will find many difficulties to overcome, for the way leads through a particularly rough section of the Cape territory. The road contains a number of short and long steep hills, the gravelly surfaces of some of which make it impossible for bicycle riding; but suppose the 'cyclist *does* make a little extra exertion, he will feel amply repaid for the work on his arrival at the journey's end, for the beach picture alone is well worth the trip to see, to say nothing of the highly enjoyable "spin" across the smooth and hard broad surface of the sandy shore.

The distance from the Gloucester Hotel to the beach is about 5½ miles. You first follow along the main highway to West Gloucester (which road has already been spoken of in a previous article), and after passing beneath the bridge at the foot of Railroad hill, take the first road leading off at the right, pointed out by the guide-board here as the way to "Coffin's Beach," and known as Concord street. The traveller soon passes the entrance to the old Presson farm on the right, then climbs the narrow stone covered hill ahead and continues on down the winding road, through a thinly populated portion of the village.

The first mile or so along this Concord street the wheelman will have a fairly good surface for his rubber-tired steed ; now and then a chance for coasting is noticed, which with due caution can be indulged in.

As the ride continues along this country path the eye meets at every turn in the way some grandly impressive picture—great hills of grey looking granite are frequently passed by—to the right now and then you catch a view of the deep blue surface of the Annisquam river and the boggy looking waters of the marshland ponds. Soon the dwelling houses become more thinly scattered and one by one drop behind, the roadway takes, if possible, a more irregular course, and then the tourist sights ahead the pleasantly situated Summer cottage of Hon. Charles P. Thompson on the left of the travelled way—a large two-story house, painted a dark red color, and sitting directly opposite the curving little lane called Atlantic street, that branches off here for Coffin's Beach. Into the narrow way last named the tourist now continues the trip, finding the road surface a trifle more difficult for easy travelling than before.

The way leads on over the rough shaggy-looking hills and around great hollows in the rocky surface made by the quarrymen in days agone, a number of deep looking gulches gaze at you from the sand covered surface further on, then the trees and tall shrubbery seem to drop behind, and a more open country comes into view.

From the top of the last high elevation over which the roadway leads, the view to the right is most magnificent. Before you is the winding Annisquam river, its deep blue surface contrasting strangely with the black, treacherous looking waters of the many pools in the marsh-lands that border the rippling stream; beyond the river is noticed a long chain of shrubbery-covered hills, that hide from our vision a glimpse of the far distant city proper.

Continuing along the route, the sight-seer soon reaches the low pasture lands that comprise a portion of the beach property; here the road leads across a swampy section, and following around the shore of a blueish-looking lake of fresh water, brings the traveller to the residence of Mr. S. T. Trumbull, the only all-year-'round inhabitant of the Coffin's Beach farm. It is but a few yards further on from Mr. Trumbull's house to the beach itself; this road is sand covered to the depth of several inches, and will have to be walked by the wheelman visitor.

Once at the beach, the picture is surveyed admiringly. Before you, if the tide is out, is a vast, almost level tract of the purest white, extending for nearly a couple of miles in length, with a width varying from a hundred feet at the narrow end to over six hundred feet at its widest point—a surface of sand firm and unyielding, that sparkles brightly under the slanting rays of a burning sun; a single object only on the white-topped plane to mar its beauty—that of the unsightly timbers of the old hulk at the far western end. To the left, as one stands facing the open sea, is noticed the high sand-covered hills, that remind the sight-seer of the snow-clad summits of the far East, and which give to the picture a most decided wintry aspect. On the right you see the 'Squam settlement, seemingly but a few rods distant, while the lighthouse in that vicinity can hardly be rec-

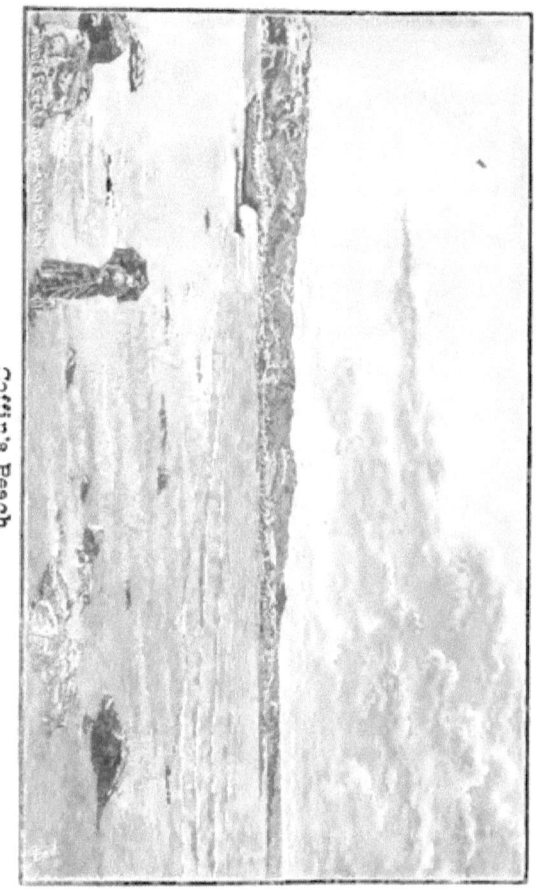

Coffin's Beach.

ognized, it seems so dwarfed and far away; beyond, you catch a glimpse of the steeples of the Bay View settlement and also of the stone sloops at the quarry piers. Fronting us is the ever restless surface of the mighty sea—you have an uninterrupted view of the entire Ipswich bay from this point, and the eye can easily follow along the coast of Newburyport and Portsmouth to the highlands of the far away Maine shores; on a clear day, and with a good glass, you can see easily the mountain Agamenticus, while the Isles of Shoals can be brought almost to your very feet.

The section known as Coffin's Beach Farm was first settled upon by one Peter Coffin in the year 1688. In extent the territory comprises nearly 500 acres, and at one time was the most valuable piece of farm land within the town's limits. Highly cultivated lands and wood covered hills gave to the region an especial importance in days long since gone by; now one looks in vain for the slightest trace of the once large dwelling of the former owner or of the house occupied by his slaves; instead of the rich looking lands and forest-crowned hills, the sight-seer notices only a collection of barren looking sand-covered hills and an uneven surface of sand-topped territory, tufted here and there with a coarse innutritous grass and dwarfed shrubbery. The present owner of the larger part of the old farm is Mr. Trumbull, before spoken of. This gentleman has recently cut up a section of the property into suitable building lots, quite a number of which have already been purchased by parties for their Summer residences; on several of these lots neat and cosy looking cottages have been erected. Mr. Trumbull built the building used as a roller-skating rink and for dancing parties, at the end of the travelled road.

In the Summer season the beach is quite a popular resort for the pleasure-loving tourist, and you are always sure of a fine dish of Trumbull's clam chowder at any time you reach the vicinity of his now famous cafe.

This property is destined some day in the near future to become one of the most popular Summer resorts along the northeast coast—as soon as the now greatly needed railroad facilities are established, and a pleasure-seeking public will not be slow in recognizing the beauties of this attractive sandy shore.

VI—MANCHESTER-BY-THE-SEA.

Seven miles from Gloucester, on the county highway leading to Salem, is the prettily situated settlement bearing the above English sounding appellation; it is another popular Summer resort for the seashore visitor, and one of the most picturesque locations on the coast. The wheelman tourist will enjoy a trip to this little village, for the route leads through an interesting section of country—the greater portion of the way being bordered with high, stately looking trees and tall densely growing shrubbery, while the gently rolling surface of the well-trodden gravelly road adds not a small portion to the pleasures of a wheel run over the country way.

From Gloucester the route extends to Magnolia, as before described, and thence over a long pleasing level surface we rapidly pedal past the large Crescent Beach Hotel and up the gently rising grade beyond, soon reaching the descending slope on the other side, down which the favorite coast takes us swiftly by the entrance to the well kept grounds of T. J. Coolidge on the left, and then around the sharp curve ahead, opposite to which is noticed the glass-like surface of a tiny lake, and way beyond the white-capped waves of the sea itself; thence the route is around the base of a wood and shrub-covered hill, whereon is noticed amid the branches the pretty cottage of the

Summer resident. On our left is a tract of meadow and farm lands, winding through which extends a narrow roadway to the homes of the seashore visitors on the hills beyond.

On over the hard road surface the wheelman now merrily spins, enjoying hugely the beautiful scenery as he wheels along. The road soon makes a curve to the left and follows up a gravelly incline to a short level section, then a couple of easy riding grades is met with, passing at this point the first guide-board pointing the way to the towns beyond. At the top of the last-mentioned hill the road winds through a thickly wooded territory, its well hardened surface adding much to the enjoyments of the ride. Now we reach a long curving descent that admits of a most delightful coast, though the cyclist should keep his feet upon the pedals until he has rounded the bend and can see the way ahead. This coast is one of the most enjoyable in all Cape Ann; you wheel rapidly through this thickly wooded section over the good surface of the country road, a deliciously cool breeze fanning you all the while; now and then you notice a finely graded and well kept way leading from the main road to the left—they are the private drive-ways of the wealthy seashore resident, and lead to as many costly villas on the coast below.

Pedaling rapidly along the now well kept road, we are soon across the railroad track and within the limits of Manchester. The road surface is excellent all along from this point, and but a few minutes are required to complete the journey to the village center.

The town of Manchester is very pleasantly situated on the north shore of Massachusetts bay. It is seven miles from Gloucester, nine miles from Salem, and about twenty-four miles from Boston over the county road. It is bounded on the north by the towns of Essex and Hamilton, on the east by Gloucester, on the south by Massachusetts bay, and on the west by the towns of Beverly and Wenham. In extent of territory the town is about four miles in length from east to west, by about two and one-half miles in breadth. Bold rocky hills and forest-covered valleys characterize the territory; the uneven surface of the township is strewn with giant bowlders and grayish looking fixed rocks; the soil is of the kind peculiar to such regions—a loomish sand mixed with a clayey substance, and the coarsest gravel. In the level sections of the town are quite a number of finely looking farms and gardens, for here the soil is well watered by numerous springs and brooks, and affords good land for cultivation.

One of the most characteristic features of the town of Manchester is the remarkable rockiness of its coast line—a feature that is especially interesting to the eye of the stranger, and the main reason why the little town has gained such high prominence as a popular Summer resort. When Mr. Dana (senior) first purchased a tract of land on the sea coast in this vicinity, in 1845, and erected a substantial looking cottage in which to pass the few months of the heated season, the desire of the wealthy in the neighboring cities to do likewise, caused a rapid rise in the valuation of the seashore property; and now one sees the result—nearly the entire section of the seashore lands has been bought up by a wealthy and cultured class, among whom are many well-known prominent people of the country; elegant costly residences have been erected, and their grounds laid out and ornamented with great taste and skill, while a large increase in the valuation of the little town has brought the tax rate down to about $4.50 per $1,000. The valuation of Manchester last year was considerably over four and a half millions; Gloucester, with its population ten times larger, had a valuation last year of but $11,376,812.

But suppose we take our wheel and pay a short visit to this interesting locality by the seashore.

We ride back toward Gloucester a few hundred feet and turn down the narrow road pointed out by the guide-board as Summer street, along which the ride now continues. We soon cross the railroad track and then climb the steep hill beyond, passing on our left, half way up the hill, the picturesque looking cottage of the veteran tragedian, Joseph Proctor; then the road winds along through a settlement of trim-looking cottages, up another short hill and on to a pleasing level roadway bordered with finely trimmed hedges and stately trees. We soon enter the private grounds of Mrs. J. H. Towne of Philadelphia, and continue over the well kept avenue to the turn-off, where a politely worded sign-board tells us that "Strangers are requested to turn here." Resting awhile at this spot, we cast our eye with delight on much of the true beauty of the locality. Before us is the vast expanse of Massachusetts bay, its surface dotted here and there with the white sails of the many swiftly gliding yachts and schooners; the white curving sandy shore ahead is the famous "Singing Beach," so named from the fact that at times the swashing sea, as it falls upon the sandy shore, sends forth a sort of musical sound that is strikingly peculiar to the listener; the large house here at this end of the beach is the residence of Mr. Wigglesworth, and it commands one of the finest views on the coast.

Returning from the Towne estate to the main highway, we take the first road leading off to the left, and again climb a short, steep hill. Now we reach a more thickly settled section, and note with pleasure the beautifully laid out grounds that sur-

IN AND AROUND CAPE ANN.

round the elegant looking dwellings. Continuing along through this pleasing settlement, we soon reach the well-known hostlery built by Mr. J. B. Booth about seven years ago, and named by him the Masconomo Hotel, in memory of an old-time chief of a once local tribe of Indians.

At the Masconomo the wheelman tourist will find a particularly agreeable host in the person of Mr. George Holliday, who has had the management of the hotel for the past few seasons; bicyclers are cordially welcomed, and may be sure of the best of treatment while under this truly hospitable roof.

The Masconomo Hotel is one of the finest on the entire Massachusetts coast. It is 240 feet in length, by over 50 feet in width, is three and a half stories in height, and has accommodations for two hundred and fifty guests. Its dining hall is 32 x 75 feet, and a large octagon hall in the centre of the house contains four mammoth fireplaces, that glow merrily with their great log fires on cold and stormy days.

The 'cycling tourist should try one of the Masconomo dinners —take the way known as Beach street, leading from the town centre to the railroad station, it is a direct road to the hotel.

From the Masconomo the run extends along the road to Manchester Neck, so called, and is through a section of much picturesque beauty. All along the route you note the many handsome looking residences, with their grounds laid out in beautiful flower beds and broad, well kept lawns; you pass the pretty chapel on the right, recently erected by Mr. Sturgis, who owns a finely built mansion in the same vicinity. Winding along, the road passes a large orchard on the left, then follows around the bend of a tiny cove that makes in here from the adjacent bay, and after climbing a rather steep incline the tourist reaches another section of the attractive settlement. The sight-seer now finds himself in the midst of a cluster of the more expensive dwellings—large, comfortable looking cottages are here very charmingly situated on this little bluff overlooking the sea, some of which are of the oddest style of architecture, and all show evidence of a lavish outlay on the part of the wealthy owner.

Continuing on over the road, you completely circle the elevated portion near the extreme point. In this vicinity you note the beautiful residence of Mr. Charles Rogers of Boston, on the hill; it is one of the most finely built mansions on the entire coast, as it is one of the most expensive. You have a magnificent view to seaward as you stand here upon the elevation—how vast the stretch of water before us seems as we gaze upon it from this point; the shore line also is plainly followed with the naked eye, even to the headlands of the distant cape beyond.

The way now leads back by a winding route, and soon the large building now in process of construction by Mr. John L. Brimmer of Boston shows itself on the left of the road. On the hill just beyond, the rambling visitor finds the cottages of Mr. Rice and J. Warren Merrill; from this standpoint the picture of the town of Manchester is particularly noticeable—it has a quiet looking appearance nestling there in the shadows of those verdure-clad hills, and seems, indeed, at peace with all the world. You notice, also, from this point, a quaint looking structure on the opposite shore of the harbor, near the bridge; it is one of the several small cottages erected by Dr. Bartol, and is called the "Barn-door" cottage, occupied this season by Mr. George A. Meyer of Boston.

The way now quickly leads the visitor into the avenue leading directly to the Masconomo (Proctor street), and soon we reach the hotel grounds. Beach street in this vicinity takes the tourist directly into the business centre of the town, and thus the circle is completed.

A number of highly enjoyable drives radiate from Manchester. One of the most interesting is to follow School street to the town of Essex—a delightful wheel run for the rambling 'cyclist; the road, after getting away from the vicinity of the dwelling houses, is bordered on either side with a thickly growing native forest, and the road surface is one of the finest for the rubber-tired wheel. A turn-off on this road at Pleasant street, on the left, will take one through a thick wood to the famous Chebacco House at the Lakes in Hamilton ; but this trip cannot be recommended as a pleasing bicycle run, for the way is rough and has a continuous run of short and long steep hills.

PART III.

I.—MISCELLANEOUS.

The hotels at Gloucester, especially recommended to the wheelman tourist and the Summer visitor, **are as follows**:

GLOUCESTER HOTEL,

on the corner of Main and Washington streets, is the regularly appointed headquarters for the C. T. C. and L. A. W. fraternity. The proprietor of the house is Mr. George L. Smith—a warm friend of the touring 'cyclist **and a genial** and painstaking host, who will exert his utmost to please his guests. Terms **are $1.50 to $2.00 per day, with** a discount **of 25** per cent. **from these prices to wheelmen.** Large parties of wheelmen intending **to visit Gloucester, should** telegraph this hotel the day before, **that the proprietor may have** everything in readiness for **them upon their arrival.**

PAVILION HOTEL,

on Western avenue, fronting the harbor, is under the management of Mr. William P. Davis—a landlord well known to former patrons of the Carleton and Everett Houses, at Jacksonville,

Pavilion Hotel, Wm. P. Davis, Proprietor.

Florida, and the Crescent Beach Hotel at Magnolia. Mr. Davis has fitted up this hotel with all the modern improvements, and is entitled to a share of the season's business.

BASS ROCK HOUSE,

at Bass Rocks, is conducted this year under the able management of Mr. F. H. Nunns (of the Quincy House, Boston). It is the L. A. W. headquarters for that section of the city; wheelmen are right at home under this hospitable roof; every room, of the seventy in the house, commands a magnificent view of land and water scenery. Terms are: for June and September, $2.00 per day; July and August, $3.00 per day. Transients, $3.50 per day. Special rates to wheelmen, according to length of visit, made known on application.

OCEAN HOUSE, Western avenue, Mrs. S. A. Sherburne, proprietor.

WEBSTER HOUSE, No. 9 Pleasant street, Nathaniel Webster, proprietor.

HESPERUS HOUSE, at Magnolia, on Hesperus avenue at the Point, Mrs. Orra Paige, manager.

OAK GROVE HOUSE, at Magnolia, on way leading off from main avenue, Mrs. B. F. Hunt, proprietor.

OCEAN-SIDE, at Magnolia, on Lexington avenue, George A. Upton, proprietor.

WILLOW COTTAGE, at Magnolia, on Magnolia avenue, Mrs. M. H. Bray, proprietor.

CRESCENT BEACH HOUSE, at Magnolia, on main highway leading to Manchester, D. S. Coffin, proprietor.

THE GRAND VIEW, at Annisquam, on Highland avenue, John S. Wyman, proprietor.

CRAIG COTTAGE, DELPHINE HOUSE, and BRAZIER COTTAGE,

at East Gloucester, are more for the permanent Summer guest than for the transient visitor.

BOSTON AND MAINE R. R. (EASTERN DIVISION.)

Station on Washington street. A. E. Elliott, ticket agent.

Summer Season, 1885. Trains leave for Boston—

From Rockport at 6.05, 7.20, 7.40, 8.30, 10.00 A. M.; 1.20, 5.00, 6.10, 9.00 P. M.

From Gloucester at 6.15, 7.29, 7.48, 8.39, 10.08 A. M.; 1.30, 5.08, 6.20, 9.09 P. M.

From Magnolia at 6.25, 7.37, 7.57, 8.46, 10.16 A. M.; 1.39, 5.17, 6.28, 9.18 P. M.

Trains leave Boston—

For Magnolia, Gloucester and Rockport, at 6.10, 8.05, 10.45 A. M.; 2.15, 3.30, 5.00, 6.20, 7.10, 9.20 P. M.

During the season of 1885 a Sunday train leaves Gloucester for Boston at 7.55 A. M.

Mr. Elliott, at this station, will cheerfully render any assistance to inquiring wheelmen. Stages connect here for Bay View, Lanesville, Essex, Annisquam and East Gloucester.

BOSTON AND GLOUCESTER STEAMBOAT CO.,

Foot of Duncan street, Gloucester, Abbott Coffin, agent; Central Wharf, Boston, E. S. Merchant, agent.

Steamers "City of Gloucester" and "George A. Chafee" leave daily—

For Boston at 3.00 and 7.45 A. M. No 3 A. M. steamer Mondays.
Leave Boston at 11.00 A. M., and 3.15 P. M. (excepting Sundays.)

During July and August, weather permitting, on Sundays boats
Leave Gloucester at 6.00 and 10.00 A. M.
Leave Boston at 3.30 P. M.

Single fare, 50 cents; commutation ticket (6 trips), $2.40.

EAST GLOUCESTER FERRY

Leaves foot of Duncan street (Parkhurst's wharf) every 15 minutes for East Gloucester.

Fare, 4 cents each way.

THE ELLIOTT SKATING RINK.

In the way of places of amusement Gloucester is sadly in want. The only really attractive section of the city in the Summer evenings is that bordering the Pavilion Beach and along the locality known as the "Cut" on Western avenue. In this vicinity there is one amusement temple that calls for especial mention here. The Elliott Skating Rink is situated nearly opposite the Pavilion Hotel; it has a skating surface 40 x 116 feet, and is the favorite resort of a large portion of our youthful populace. The proprietor is Mr. Smith, of the L. A. W. hotel, and he has proven a most energetic one, with the able assistance of his manager, Mr. Fred. A. Harbison. A specialty at this place is a series of social dancing parties, on Saturday evenings —it is just the place to pass a pleasant two-hours for our wheelman visitors.

THE CAPE ANN YACHT CLUB.

As many visitors come to Gloucester during the Summer months that are either more or less interested in the yachting matters of the city, I have obtained from the secretary of our local club a list of the several boats over 15 feet water-line, belonging to that organization, together with their respective sizes, rig, and owner's name, as appears on the following page :

NAME.	OWNER.	KEEL OR C. B.	RIG.	Length Over All	WATER-LINE.
Sparkle	G. W. Patterson	Keel	Sch.	41.06	37.02
Forrest Bickford	J. F. Bickford	C. B.	Sloop	29.06	27.00
Three Sisters	G. A. Douglass	C. B.	Sloop	28.09	26.06
Effie Everett	J. F. Bickford	Keel	Sloop	27.08	25.03
Venus	W. McKenzie	C. B.	Sloop	26.05	23.06
Black Cloud	Brown & Wheeler	C. B.	Sloop	26.06	22.10
Roldon	F. F. Martin	C. B.	Sloop	22.05	21.10
Adele	Haskell Bros.	C. B.	Sloop	23.07	20.10
Kittiwake	C. E. Cunningham	C. B.	Cat	21.10	20.10
Charm	G. Wheeler	Keel	Sloop	22.07	20.07
Tarquin	J. E. Smothers	C. B.	Sloop	22.10	20.00
Fatinitza	F. Norwood	C. B.	Sloop	21.05	20.00
Kate	J. McLoughlin	Keel	Sloop	19.10	19.01
Marguerite	J. McLaughlin	C. B.	Sloop	18.06	18.02
Hestia	W. Dennen	C. B.	Sloop	20.03	17.09
Jennie C.	H. A. Lane	C. B.	Cat	18.03	16.07
Sassacus	B. Griffin	C. B.	Sloop	18.05	16.03
Spark	F. H. Gaffney	C. B.	Sloop	20.00	16.02
Two Brothers	Higgins & Gifford	C. B.	Cat	16.04	15.06

This Club has about sixty members and twenty-five yachts, and is quite a healthy organization. The Club was organized July 28, 1880, and the following are its officers for 1885:

Commodore, Bennett Griffin; *Vice Commodore*, Frank H. Gaffney; *Treasurer*, Frank E. Smothers; *Secretary and Measurer*, H. Frank Sanford; *Fleet Captain*, John F. Bickford; *Trustees*, Bennett Griffin, Frank H. Gaffney, William McKenzie.

II—A WHEEL RUN IN '78.

NOTE.—The following sketch of a run made by the author in the early days of bicycling, was written for the columns of a juvenile weekly, and first appeared in the winter of 1879. I give it place here as of more or less interest, with a few slight alterations.

The City Hall clock was just pointing to eight, on as fine a morning as one could wish to enjoy a bicycle spin, and the roads looked their very best after the slight rain-fall of the evening before, as the writer and a companion, "Tommy," made their first vault upon their respective "pig-skins," preparatory to a run of forty miles, and a day's enjoyment. My machine was a Pope "Columbia" of the Excelsior pattern, and was the first bicycle introduced into this city; it was half-nickle plated, and measured fifty-two inches across its forward wheel; it had been my pride for many weeks, and I was warmly attached to it—in fact, I often remarked that five hundred dollars would not tempt me to part with my "wheel," were another machine unobtainable. The saddle was a "patent suspension" a pear-shaped piece of cast iron, hollowed out, and covered with a tightly-drawn piece of "pig-skin," and was the easiest in use. Attached to the rear of the machine, and just beneath the projecting end of the saddle, was a small leathern bag, containing our sundries —oil can, wrench, key, chain, rag, etc.

My companion bestrode a similar patterned machine, though of smaller size. Tommy was a splendid rider, and one I always watched with envy—he could make his fifty miles and scarcely show the cost in the way of "wind."

Well, all this time we have been gliding along "in our noiseless flight," with the town of Beverly, our destination, fourteen miles ahead. We kept up a spirited conversation, and now and then attempted the "fancy" on the broad and well trodden track. But here we are at the summit of a long hill, with a descent before us, foretelling lively riding, and ere I think we are already upon its surface, and like the wind itself go tearing down the irregular course. Such fun, boys! Get a bicycle, by all means—my word for it, you will never regret its purchase. Continuing on over level ground, up and down steep ascents and falling grades, taking the sidewalk here and there, we finally reach Manchester, one hour from the start, and seven miles on our journey.

At Manchester we carefully oil our machines, give them the customary "shake," to see if "all is well," and then again secure our balance and resume the ride.

Good roads are found all along our route from this place, save a short and gravelly hill as we enter Beverly Farms. I was in advance of Tommy as we were nearing this hill, and intending to ride to the top, glanced back over my shoulder to look for my companion, when my wheel struck a great mound of loose gravel, and over I went to the ground.

We had a most delightful run through Beverly Farms. Here we found an unusually fine road, and over it we rapidly wheeled to Pride's Crossing, where again we tested the racing qualities of our slender wheels to the fullest extent. I held the advance for about a quarter of a mile, then Tommy overtook and passed me like a flash, and in a few minutes I was a considerable distance in the rear.

Just as I was about to whistle to my companion, I noticed him suddenly spring to the ground and allow his bicycle to fall over with him, and the next instant I saw coming around the bend and directly in my path, a runaway horse attached to a basket phaeton, in which latter two elderly gentlemen were seated.

On came the affrighted animal, till he caught sight of me as I still sat upon my machine and continued my silent advance, then, apparently taking me for an apparition, sprang with forward feet upon the high stone wall running along the highway, and came to a stop, his entire body covered with a thick white foam. I at once dismounted and went to the assistance of the occupants of the carriage, saying as I approached :

"Any damage?"

I received no answer to this, and after waiting a while spoke again :

"Anything I can do for you?"

At last I seemed to have been heard, for the gentleman whom I saw had been driving, turned to me and said :

"Young man, why do you desecrate the Sabbath by riding such a machine?"

I had forgotten to tell you, boys, that this trip was being made on Sunday. Now I don't say but what I might have selected a day just as well suited to the occasion, but it's awful hard to allow a fine Sunday to pass and not take a little ramble with your bicycle, if you are so fortunate as to own one.

I told the gentleman, in reply to his question, that I did not quite understand him.

"I should think six days enough to take out of the week for

practicing upon a bicycle, without calling upon the seventh," he continued, apparently shocked at my seeming ignorance.

"Well, then," said I, boldly, "why do you take your carriage out to-day—for pleasure? Exactly."

This remark settled it quickly. The gentleman (?) did not even look at me, but gathered up the reins, spoke a word to the now quieted horse, and started off down the road, and I saucily sent a parting "Good-day, sir!" after him.

I walked with my machine to where Tommy sat awaiting me, from whence he had witnessed the whole affair, and together we had a most hearty laugh over the matter. "Of all 'nerve,'" said my companion, "I never saw the like of that"; and I agreed with him. Well, thank goodness, the wheelman does not meet with many such characters; on the contrary, most people, especially those of an observing nature, seem to enjoy the graceful movements of the slender wheel as much as the rider himself.

Well, once more astride the rubber-tired wheel, we continue our trip and soon arrive in the town of Beverly. At this place, beneath the shade of an inviting looking maple, we take a rest of perhaps thirty minutes, and enjoy our cigarettes; then a careful examination of our machines is made—a nut adjusted here and there, and the saddle moved slightly to the front—after which the remount is taken for an eight-mile run to Wenham, Hamilton, and the Chebacco Lakes. This run was the poorest of the entire trip, all hills and a road surface of deep gravel—two very disagreeable items the bicycler always expects to meet. We did not dismount but once, however, and this occurred at the junction of the roads leading to Hamilton, Beverly and Manchester. We found a nice road running alongside the Pond—a good hard surface with several highly enjoyable coasts, away to the Chebacco Pond hotel—and on this we made up our lost time. We were just one hour in making the distance from Beverly, and considering the state of the roads it was very good time indeed.

Well, now, we did enjoy that dinner at Whipple's! What an appetite we did have as we sat down to that well-spread table. A single chicken we made nothing of—you should have seen the way we tucked the cream toast, squash pie, cake, fruits, nuts and candy out of sight.

I was beginning to feel "dubious" about getting home, when Tommy called my attention to the fact that it was five o'clock, and knowing a long run awaited us, we finished supper and went out doors to prepare for our long ride home. At precisely 5.55 P. M. we left the Chebacco House and headed for Beverly Farms, and the long home stretch of about twenty miles, and at eight o'clock reached Gloucester safely, well satisfied with our first long-distance run upon the bicycle.

III — WHEELMAN VISITORS IN PAST YEARS.

From the time of the first appearance of the rubber-tired wheel in America until the present year, the trip along the north shore to Gloucester, Massachusetts, has been considered one of the most enjoyable wheel-runs in all New England. The first visit of the bicycle to Gloucester was in the early part of the year 1878. The writer well remembers the curious crowd of lookers-on that surrounded the pioneer wheelman as the dismount was made on the main thoroughfare of the town; even now the many questions and exclamations of the wonder-struck populace can be recalled to mind, as they gazed with mouth agape upon the slender two-wheeled team. The rider came from Cambridge, Mass., and made the trip in three and a quarter hours; the machine was a 54-inch English make affair, and was a heavy, clumsy-looking wheel in comparison with the beautiful models of to-day. The wheelman made the return journey by train.

Messrs. Paul Butler and Willis Farrington, both of Lowell, Mass., (who with four others founded the Boston Bicycle Club in February of this year) were among the early visitors to this city, on wheels; their favorite run being to Gloucester, thence to Ipswich and Newburyport, and along the wooded roads of Essex county.

IN AND AROUND CAPE ANN.

The first notable event was the visit of the

WALTHAM BICYCLE CLUB, AUGUST, 1880.

This party consisted of four wheelmen, namely—C. W. Sewall, Captain; Fred. E. Draper, Sec'y; W. W. Stall and Lewis Damareau. A cordial reception was tendered the visitors by Messrs. C. S. Nauss, Lewis Fewkes (both members of the club, then on a visit to the city), A. F. Dodd and the writer. It was exactly 9.30 in the evening when the 'cyclists were met at the Cut bridge, and the moon was shining brightly. The visitors were conducted to the residence of Mr. Nauss on Marchant street, where a most appetizing fish chowder was partaken of, after which the ride was continued to the store of A. F. Dodd on Main street, where the final dismount was made and the machines stabled. Sunday was pleasantly passed by the visiting 'cyclists in a trip down the harbor to Eastern Point, through the courtesy of Mr. Dodd. The return trip was begun at 4.30 P. M., on Main street, before a large crowd of lookers-on, and the visitors left for their long run, well pleased with their first visit to this city. Stall rode a 58-inch wheel and Sewall a 46-inch.

MASSACHUSETTS BICYCLE CLUB, SEPT. 15, 1880.

Messrs. C. A. Hazlett (Rockingham Bi. Club, Portsmouth, N. H.), E. W. Pope (Capt. Mass. Bi. Club, Boston), and A. J. Philbrick (Salem), visited Gloucester Sept. 11, 1880, for the purpose of making arrangements for a three days' run of the Massachusetts Bicycle Club, and on Sept. 15 this Club came to town and passed the night at the Pavilion Hotel. In this party were the following well-known wheelmen: E. W. Pope, H. E. Parkhurst, A. F. Webster (Massachusetts Club, Boston); J. M. Baines and Thomas Earll (Worcester Bi. Club); S. T. Cook and

C. White (Baltimore, Md., Club); Capt. C. K. Munroe (N. Y. Bi. Club); W. F. Gullen (Brooklyn Bi. Club); C. A. Hazlett and A. H. Jenness (Rockingham Club, Portsmouth, N. H.); W. D. Wilmot (the great fancy rider—this was his first long ride, and he then belonged to the Framingham Club); J. G. Dalton (Boston Bi. Club); and Messrs. W. E. Parmenter, Jr., and George E. Riley. The party were met at Magnolia by local riders, A. F. Dodd and the writer, and escorted to the hotel. In the early morning the wheelmen were photographed at the Pavilion by W. A. Elwell, and at 7.15 the party left via Essex for the journey home.

Messrs. Hazlett and Pope, with Capt. Williams and W. S. Slocum, again visited town Sept. 15 of the next year, and on the 18th of the same month the former, with President Frank J. Philbrick of the Rockingham Club, made the run from Nashua, N. H., to this city, each time passing the night at the Pavilion hotel.

THE BOSTON BICYCLE CLUB, JULY, 1881,

made a trip to this city via steamer "Admiral," and were met at the wharf by local wheelmen C. F. Wonson and the writer, and escorted to the Pavilion, where the night was passed. The party numbered fourteen wheelmen, including Frank W. Weston (Chief Consul U. S. A. of the C. T. C.) and Mr. Louis R. Harrison, then late editor of the *Bicycling World.* On Sunday morning the trip home was begun on wheels, local riders accompanying the visitors as far as Magnolia. One of the party (now a prominent official in one of the leading 'cycle clubs at the Hub) had the good fortune to make the acquaintance of a dark-eyed damsel of the town, and deserted his party for a carriage drive in her company, to a well-spread dinner table at the Chebacco Lakes.

IN AND AROUND CAPE ANN.

MASSACHUSETTS BICYCLE CLUB, OCT. 26-27, 1881,

again made the trip to this city. Local riders welcomed the visitors at Magnolia and escorted them to the L. A. W. headquarters of the town—Gloucester Hotel (then Atlantic House). This party consisted of the following: H. H. Williams, Captain; H. L. Sanborn, Color Bearer; G. W. Metcalf, Bugler; Aug. F. Webster, M. H. Hardwick, Dr. H. A. Boker, S. T. Parker, L. M. Dorr, H. E. Parkhurst, J. T. Dyer, A. J. Philbrick, Samuel Kidder, Albert S. Parsons, W. R. Griffiths (all of Massachusetts Club); Fred. S. Pratt and Waldo Lincoln (Worcester Club); L. R. Harrison, J. G. Dalton and C. W. Fourdrinier (Boston Club); Frank J. Philbrick (Rockingham Club, Portsmouth, N. H.); W. T. Gilman, (Nashua Club). The evening was very pleasantly passed in the parlor of the hotel, Mr. Parkhurst entertaining the company with selections on the piano. Mr. H. A. Burnham, the *Herald* man of the town, also did considerable toward making the evening one of much enjoyment to the visiting wheelmen. The ride back next morning was by the way of Essex, North Beverly and Middlesex Fells to Boston, and the distance covered in the two days' run was one hundred and three miles.

STAR BICYCLE CLUB, LYNN, MAY, 1882,

came to Gloucester with seven members, viz.: Frank S. Winship, J. Horace Pope, Walter O. Faulkner, Will C. Stewart, W. E. Smith, Frank Goodwin and William Pevear, and put up at the L. A. W. hotel. The day was warm and sunny, and the roads were in fine condition. A very clever performance was the feat of riding up Sawyer's hill at the Cove, by one of the wheelmen of the Star Club; this was the first time the hill had been ridden on a bicycle, and was considered a most difficult undertaking. Since this year (1882) the road surface of the hill has been somewhat improved, and now the task is comparatively easy for the wheelman to make a successful mount.

In the month of August, 1882, Messrs. W. B. Everett, J. F. Souther, George W. Page and E. Westcott, took a flying trip on wheels to this city and passed the night, returning next day to Boston.

RAMBLERS BICYCLE CLUB, BOSTON, JUNE, 1883.

Probably the greatest event in the annals of the bicycling history of Gloucester was the visit of the Ramblers Club, of Boston, in their two-days' run from that city, June 17, 18, 1883. This party numbered twenty-nine wheelmen, and was the largest touring body to visit this city. Henry Parsons of this city, and the writer met the 'cyclists at Salem, and came over the road from that place with the visitors, putting up here at the L. A. W. hotel. The Hawthorne Club of Salem, under command of Capt. Philbrick, did escort duty to Manchester, and then the Gloucester wheelmen assumed that post and brought the tourists into the town. Next morning the 'cyclists visited Bass Rocks at East Gloucester, and were greatly pleased with the locality; a couple of hours were here passed, during which a fine photograph of the wheelmen was taken by Adams, of Gloucester, and then the visitors returned to the hotel. Several of the party left at 12 o'clock, returning via wheel to Salem, and the rest took the 1.30 P. M. train. The following were the members on the entire trip: H. R. Reed, C. S. Howard, W. P. Haskell, Albert L. Flocken, W. I. Harris, A. D. Peck, Jr., W. S. Locke, J. W. Wattles, Jr., H. M. Smith, A. W. Fisher, F. E. Bryant, Elmer G. Whitney, W. E. Webber (Ramblers); Fred.

A. Bickford, J. D. Bullard, Fred. C. Fitz and W. M. Welch (all of Somerville Bicycle Club); J. L. Blackmer (Roxbury Club); J. J. Gilligan (Massachusetts Club); E. E. Gage (Hyde Park); E. P. J. Morton (Melrose); F. A. Hill, J. C. Freeman, Elias Ahuja, W. B. Dyer and F. P. Martin (unattached); P. H. Shirley (Marblehead Club); F. A. Woodman and R. T. Farnum (Chelsea Bi. Club).

On Sunday, July 21, 1883, Messrs. E. P. J. Morton and J. J. Gilligan, in company with the writer, made the run from Gloucester to Chebacco Pond, and partook of a Whipple dinner of broiled chickens.

August 12, 1883, Messrs. John Z. Rogers, F. W. Farnham, Wm. M. Foster and T. L. Scanall, were the wheelmen visitors.

August 18, 1883, Herbert M. Smith, George E. Hutchinson, George E. Butterfield, Willard E. Butterfield, Joseph L. Pearson and M. L. Collins were the arrivals on wheels.

Sept. 6, 1883, E. H. Gilman (Nashua, N. H.), William F. Ford (Boston, Mass.), J. W. DeWolf (Cambridge) and Frank C. Hoyt Springfield, Mass.), came to town from Newton, Mass., on wheels; next morning DeWolf wheeled to Cambridge and the two former to Nashua, N. H. J. Fred. Adams of Haverhill also paid a flying visit to Gloucester the same week, making the distance of twenty-eight miles in three hours.

Sept. 22, 1883. The visitors this day included a delegation from the now well-known Charlestown Club, under command of the genial Captain, Charles W. Howard—F. A. Parshley, J. W. Vivian, F. S. Nelson, J. A. Webber, W. H. Davis, Arthur R. Smith, Frank S. Mason and Cliff. M. Bean. This party had a most enjoyable time and kept the city wide-awake during their visit.

October 6, 1883, representatives of the East Boston Club were entertained, viz: John C. Soutter, William C. Moore, F. H. Brewster, Thomas C. Coleman, T. H. Kingston, J. L. Blackman and Herman Reed.

October 13, 1883, H. M. Smith and W. E. Webber of the Ramblers Club, Boston.

November 18, 1883, C. W. Howard and J. W. Vivian of the Charlestown Club, and

November 17, 1883, E. G. Whitney (Ramblers), F. A. Woodman, and G. H. Danforth (Chelsea Club), completed the list of visiting wheelmen for 1883.

During the year 1884 Messrs. E. P. J. Morton and J. J. Gilligan were frequent visitors to Gloucester, and later, Messrs. Woodman and Danforth of Chelsea passed a whole fortnight in pleasing wheel-runs in this city. Benj. F. Eddy of Melrose was an occasional visitor this year, and indulged in many of the enjoyable trips upon the Cape.

October, 1884, the Charlestown Club again organized one of their pleasing tours to Cape Ann; this time over thirty wheelmen participated in the run, representing clubs from Cambridge, Charlestown, East Boston, Chelsea and Wakefield. The party came to town of a Saturday night by train and boat, and quartered at the Gloucester Hotel. During the evening the Elliott Rink was visited, and here the wheelmen tendered a most cordial reception to Dan Canary, the trick rider, who at that time was fulfilling an engagement with the Girard & Vokes Combination. A "Kangaroo" wheel was introduced to the Gloucester people by this party, and its rider, Mr. William E. Webber, gave an excellent exhibition of skilful riding at the skating rink. The party left at 9.30 in the morning, and were accompanied as far as Pride's Crossing, by the writer. The "headers" were quite numerous on the trip, and one rider wrenched his machine badly in descending Sawyer's hill.

The writer timed Still. Whittaker here, this month, on his one-hundred mile run. Whittaker made remarkably fast time on this run, and broke the previous record. He left Harvard square in Cambridge at 7 A. M., and rode to Wellesley and return (22 miles), thence to Salem and return (62 miles), thence to Gloucester (99 miles). reaching this city at 3.50 P. M. Some one suggested that he had hardly covered the one hundred miles, and to fully satisfy the party, and more probably himself, Whittaker rode out to the schoolhouse on the Manchester road ($1\frac{3}{4}$ miles) and returned to the Gloucester Hotel at exactly 4 P. M., giving him a full one hundred miles, with one and a-half to spare. Whittaker looked fairly well, and no doubt could have returned to Cambridge on the wheel had he been so disposed. He left on the 5.08 P. M. train, after sending a telegram to the Club house at Harvard square.

E. P. J. Morton (Mass. Bi. Club), F. A. Woodman and G. H. Danforth (Chelsea) were among the first arrivals the present year. April 25 was the date, and the wheelmen were obliged to pass the entire next day in-doors on account of a heavy rain, and returned on Monday morning via 6.20 train.

May 16, Messrs. L. F. Frost and F. A. Woodman of Chelsea were here for the night, and returned next morning on the wheel.

May 30, a large party visited town, including the following: A. J. Rogers, William Bell, T. C. Coleman, Ralph Hahn, Charles E. Little. F. H. Brewster, William C. Moore, C. G. Schwan, F. J. Libbee, C. C. Curin and E. Kingston (Maverick Wheel Club, East Boston); J. H. Aubin, P. L. Aubin, W. G. Clark, A. A.

Glimes, F. L. Tainter, W. E. Wentworth (Newton); R. G. Beazley (Boston); E. Frost, R. H. Loud, B. W. Hobbs, A. D. Guver, W. Jordan, George S. Webster (East Boston); George A. Minott and W. W. Merrick (Lynn); and J. R. Harmer (East Hartford). A disagreeable rain-storm kept the party in town the following day, and the home trip was made next morning by the early train.

June 14, another delegation passed the night in this city, as follows: W. W. White, F. Arthur Lane, J. W. Vivian (Charlestown Club); G. H. Danforth, F. A. Woodman (Chelsea); H. S. Worthen (Capt.), W. R. Maxwell (V. Pres.), G. F. Steele (Sec.), Eugene Sanger (1st Lieut.), E. Ames (Somerville Cycle Club); Benj. F. Eddy, and E. P. J. Morton—the former of Melrose and the latter a Massachusetts Club man. The following day (Sunday), Messrs. Lane, Danforth, Woodman, Eddy and Morton, under the guidance of the writer, took the famous " Wheel around the Cape." The day was fine, though the wheelmen had a stiff breeze to ride against on the last eight or ten miles. E. P. J. Morton was the only man in the party to ride up Great Hill, and especial mention is due that gentleman for his very clever performance.

July 4, a party of twenty-eight, representing the East Boston, Newton and Charlestown Clubs, were in town over night, most of the visitors coming via the Boston & Gloucester steamer in the afternoon. And here our record closes for the year.

In the foregoing I have not attempted to give a complete list of the visiting wheelmen in the several years—simply selected the most prominent parties, and important club runs, for the sake of having a convenient list for future reference—hence those of the wheelmen tourists who fail to find their names in the preceding pages, will kindly understand that the omission was not in any way on account of their not being worthy honorable mention, but from the fact that want of space alone prevented their publication.

THE END.

www.ingramcontent.com/pod-product-compliance
Lightning Source LLC
Chambersburg PA
CBHW020133170426
43199CB00010B/730